The Ultimate Prize

The Ultimate Prize

Great Christian Olympians

Stuart Weir

Hodder & Stoughton
LONDON SYDNEY AUCKLAND

First published in Great Britain in 2004

British Library Cataloguing in Publication Data
A record for this book is available from the British Library

ISBN 0 340 86225 4

Typeset in Bembo by Avon DataSet Ltd,
Bidford-on-Avon, Warwickshire

Printed and bound in Great Britain by
Bookmarque Ltd, Croydon, Surrey

The paper and board used in this paperback are natural recyclable
products made from wood grown in sustainable forests.
The manufacturing processes conform to the environmental
regulations of the country of origin.

Hodder & Stoughton
A Division of Hodder Headline Ltd
338 Euston Road
London NW1 3BH
www.madaboutbooks.com

To Lynne, who, to quote Wray Vamplew, 'puts sport in its proper perspective, but who still understands how important it is to me'.

Contents

1

The Games in Historical Perspective

The Olympics remain unique as a sporting event. Held every four years, the Olympic Games represent the pinnacle of sporting achievement, and athletes sacrifice everything in the preceding four-year period for the chance of winning a medal, or even just for the honour of taking part. The Olympics, more than any other sporting event, have managed to find a place for the true amateur, the representative of the tiny nation alongside the millionaire superstar American sprinter.

The Olympics have an unrivalled pedigree. They began in 776 BC in Greece, and are the clearest expression of the origin of organised sport. Then, as now, the Games gathered competitors together on one site and integrated sport into a wider festival. Right from their origin, the Games were taken very seriously; and youths in Sparta were taken from their families and reared in austere conditions in preparation for combat, the forerunner of the modern training camp.

In fact, there is more in common between the ancient Games and the modern ones than one might expect. From these early times, competitors were supported during their training, and the successful ones were richly rewarded when they returned to their home towns. The announcement of the festival itself was made about a year in advance, inviting entries from all over Greece; however, only free-born Greeks could compete. Competitors undertook to train for 10 months, of which the last one would be spent in the gymnasium at Olympia.

Founded on Mount Olympia, far from Sparta, Corinth and Athens, the origin of the Olympic Games is shrouded in mystery and legend. According to one legend, Hercules founded the Games to celebrate his own feats. Another legend is that they commemorate Zeus's victory over Cronus. Then there is the legend of Pelops, which claims that he won his bride in a chariot escapade. It is perhaps significant that all these legends involve aggression, competition and victory. The ancient Greeks believed that the body and the mind required discipline, and that those who mastered this discipline would best honour the god Zeus. They referred to this discipline as a 'marriage of mind and muscle'.

Whatever the exact origin of the Games, the link to Zeus is undeniable as Olympia was made a shrine to Zeus in 1000 BC, and young Greeks competed as an act of worship to this god. While today's athletes have accommodation provided for them in an Olympic village, it was not until 350 BC that any sort of shelter was provided for the competitors. Before that, it was normal for athletes to sleep in the open air.

Up to 50,000 male spectators would watch the Games and engage in religious ceremonies, and the lighting of a flame at the altar of Zeus marked the opening of the event. When the Games ended, the flame was extinguished.

The modern Olympic opening ceremony can be traced back to ancient times. The spectators at the ancient Games would have watched a procession of priests and officials, of animals for sacrifice, of athletes, chariots and horses. Ambassadors from many states were also present. As each competitor passed the VIP rostrum, the herald would announce his name, his father's name and his city of origin. Then the festival would commence with the sacrifice of the animals on the altar of Zeus.

The Olympic festival took place in August or September. This was a hot and dry time of the year, a time when the farmers were not at their busiest and, therefore, were able to attend the Games.

Women were banned – on pain of death – from even attending the Games, and the historian Pausanias tells the story of Pherenice, who was so desperate to see her son compete that she disguised herself as a trainer and took a place in the stadium. When her son won, in her excitement she jumped a barrier, fell, and was revealed to be a woman. She narrowly escaped death, but the rules were thereafter changed to specify that in future all trainers must, like the athletes, be naked.

Alongside the sporting festival, there was a significant 'fringe festival', with authors reading from their books, sculptors exhibiting their art, and poets seeking commissions to immortalise the victors. There was fun and entertainment, with food and drink for sale, and the whole area was turned into a tented village.

The first Games consisted of only one race, but gradually others were introduced, then the pentathlon, wrestling, boxing and chariot races. From 632 BC onwards, however, the Games became more organised, lasting five days. To be more precise, the festival lasted five days, with the Games themselves only taking two and a half. The first day was the opening ceremony, with oaths, prayers, sacrifices and hymn singing.

Competition began on day two, with chariot races and equestrian events. This second day started with the sacrifice of a ram in honour of Pelops, and in the afternoon it was the pentathlon: discus, javelin, standing jump, 200m and wrestling. If a contestant won three events, he was instantly declared the overall champion, and the pentathletes were much admired for their combination of strength and speed.

On day three were the foot-races from 200m to 4800m, and day four was given over to the heavy events: wrestling, boxing, armoured foot-races, etc. Day five was taken up with the prize-giving and feasting.

Dio Chrysostom, quoted by H. A. Harris in *Greek Athletes and Athletics* (Hutchinson, 1967, p. 139), describes the Isthmian Games in the first century as follows. (While the Isthmian Games are not the Olympics, it seems likely that this would be an accurate picture of the atmosphere around the Olympics too.)

> Then round the temple of Poseidon you could see and hear the accursed sophists shouting and abusing one another, and their so-called pupils fighting with each other, many authors giving readings of their works which no one listens to, many poets reciting their poems and others expressing approval of them, many conjurors performing their tricks and many fortune-tellers interpreting omens, thousands of lawyers arguing cases, a host of cheap-jacks selling everything under the sun.

When Christianity became the official religion of the Roman empire, Christians insisted that all pagan temples be closed, and in AD 393–4 the religious rites associated with the ancient Olympics were severed, by order of the Christian Roman emperor, Theodosius. This closed the sanctuary and the Games gradually died out. Then in 522 and 551 two massive earthquakes levelled the temple and changed the course of the River Cronus, washing the Hill of Cronus down into the valley.

Signs of interest in reviving the Games were first seen in Britain in the seventeenth century when Robert Dover started the Olympick Games in Chipping Camden in 1612. They included running, equestrian events, wrestling, hunting, coursing and throwing, as well as a cultural festival. The Games then continued until 1852 when they were banned for 'rowdiness and dangerous activities'.

In 1850 William Penny Brookes, a Shropshire doctor, had started the Wenlock Games at Much Wenlock, which included traditional English sports; and when Baron Pierre de Coubertin (born in Paris in 1863) became concerned about the state of French education, and wanted to introduce an element of physical education into France, he visited Much Wenlock. He was impressed by what he found and also became intrigued by the development of sport in English public schools, through the influence of the 'Muscular Christianity' movement.

De Coubertin first proposed the idea of the modern Olympics in 1892 and spent the next three years getting support for the idea. He held an international conference in Paris in 1893, where 12 countries were represented and another 21 wrote to express support for his ideas. This conference formed the International Olympic Committee (IOC), and the modern Olympic movement had been born, with the first Games being set for 1896. De Coubertin regarded the opening and closing ceremonies as a vital part of the Olympics, without which the Olympics would just be 'another World Championship'.

Athens 1896

Thus the first 'modern Olympics' took place in April 1896 in Athens. There were 245 participants from 14 countries – 9 sports and 43 events (compared to 10,000 participants, 200 countries, 25-plus sports and nearly 300 events in the twenty-first century). King George I of Greece declared the Games open. When the decision was taken in 1894 to hold the Games in Athens, 15 sports were proposed. However, this proved unrealistic and only nine survived to make the programme of the first Games. Some of the more bizarre events included one-handed weightlifting, and 100m freestyle swimming for members of the Greek navy – in the sea off Piraeus. Winners were awarded silver medals.

Fittingly, a Greek shepherd called Spiridon Louis was the hero of these Games, winning the marathon – a race that commemorated the legend of Pheidippides, the man who allegedly carried news of the Greek victory at the Battle of the

Marathon in 490 BC by running all the way from Marathon to Athens.

While the athletic standards were modest at the early Games, the enthusiasm and good sportsmanship of the Greek spectators ensured the success of the event.

Paris 1900

If Athens was the appropriate location for the first modern Olympics because of the Greek legacy, then Paris was appropriate in 1900 because France was the homeland of Baron Pierre de Coubertin, the actual founder of the modern Olympics. However, there were those who felt that the modern Olympics, like the ancient, should be permanently held in Greece.

By 1900, the number of participants had grown to 1225, including, for the first time, 19 women. The number of countries represented was 26 and there were 166 events. One ludicrous aspect of the Paris games was that they lasted from May to October! They were also reduced to a mere appendage of the World Exhibition taking place in Paris that same year.

The swimming events were notable for producing some outstanding times – mainly because they were held in the River Seine, swimming with the current! The Games closed with no ceremony and several competitors went away from their events not knowing who had won. For example, the American Margaret Abbott won a nine-hole golf tournament, but died in 1955 without realising that it had been an Olympic event!

Another interesting feature of the 1900 Games was the introduction of five team-sports – tennis, football, polo, rowing and tug-of-war – in which teams from different countries competed. The 1900 programme also included some unusual one-off events, including the equestrian high jump and long jump, and the swimming obstacle race, which required competitors to climb a pole, scramble over boats, and then swim under them! Professionals were allowed to compete in some events and also receive cash prizes.

Several American' competitors, though, withdrew from their events when they discovered that they were scheduled for a Sunday.

St Louis 1904

The 1904 Olympics in St Louis were a mixed success. Again, they lasted six months, but the location meant that less than half as many nations were represented as in 1900. In St Louis there were only 687 participants from 13 countries, 6 sports and 104 events. However, only 84 of these events are generally agreed to have been Olympic events and, of them, only half included a non-American competitor. The year 1904 saw gold, silver and bronze medals awarded for the first time.

The contribution to Olympic history of the 1904 Games was to add the 'plunge for distance' event. In this, contestants dived into the swimming pool, remained motionless for 60 seconds or until their head broke the surface of the water, when they had their distance measured. The winner was William Dickey with 19.05 metres. One wonders why the event didn't catch on!

In fact, St Louis was lucky to host the Games at all. They had been awarded to Chicago, but as St Louis was the venue of the Louisiana Purchase Exhibition, a kind of world fair, President Theodore Roosevelt decided to transfer the Games to St Louis to avoid the possibility of the two events competing with each other in different cities.

An interim Olympic Games was then held in Greece in 1906, to revive the Olympic spirit after the problems of 1900 and 1904. They were, however, not awarded official status.

London 1908

The 1908 Games were originally scheduled for Rome and Naples, in Italy, but Mount Vesuvius had other intentions and erupted at an inconvenient moment. London was the second choice, and within 10 months a stadium had been built at Shepherd's Bush, which included a running track, cycling track, football field, swimming pool and facilities for gymnastics and wrestling. Compare that with the problems we have had with the New Wembley stadium and Pickett's Lock debacle!

The marathon captured the imagination of the crowd and remained in the memory of spectators, as Dorando Pietri of Italy entered the stadium way ahead of the field only to collapse five times, eventually having to be helped over the line, which meant he was disqualified.

There were 2035 participants – although only 36 women – from 22 countries, 21 sports and 110 events; and for the first time at the opening ceremony, athletes marched into the stadium by nation.

Stockholm 1912

Electronic timing for events was introduced for the first time in Stockholm, and the 'Athlete of the Games' was undoubtedly Jim Thorpe of the USA. He won the pentathlon, came fourth in the high jump, seventh in the long jump, and finally won the decathlon with a points score that would have won him the silver medal up until 1948. The top four in the men's 800m all broke the world record, while Gottfried Fuchs of Germany scored an incredible 10 goals in a consolation football match against Russia.

The Games were now stabilising in size with 2547 participants, 28 countries, 13 sports and 102 events.

Sweden refused to allow boxing, and this led to a change in procedures, with the international committee, rather than the local organising one, having the final say in what sports were included in the programme. Following this, the IOC decided to distinguish between three categories of sport. There were the primary individual sports, which had to be included in every Olympic Games; the second category was mandatory team sports; and the third was optional sports, whereby the local organising committee had discretion as to their inclusion.

Berlin 1916

The 1916 Games were scheduled for Berlin, but were cancelled due to the outbreak of war. This was in stark contrast to ancient Greece, where the practice was to suspend wars to allow the Games to proceed.

Antwerp 1920

The first Olympics after the First World War were beset by difficulties, and numbers were depleted with the banning of Germany, Austria, Hungary, Bulgaria and Turkey. The Games were also hit by financial problems. Antwerp was chosen as the venue, partly to recognise that Belgium had suffered arguably more devastation in the First World War than any other country.

The Athlete of the Games was Nedo Nadi of Italy, who won five gold medals in six fencing events, a feat still unequalled. (His was a talented family as his brother won four medals.) Suzanne Lenglen won the Olympic tennis women's singles, losing just four games in 10 sets. For the first and only time, ice-hockey was included in the Summer Games.

A new Olympic pledge was introduced in 1920: 'In the name of all competitors, I promise that we will take part in these Olympic Games, respecting and abiding by the rules which govern them, in the true spirit of sportsmanship, for the glory of sport and the honour of our teams.'

Paris 1924

The Paris Olympics in 1924 were, in a way, a tribute to Baron de Coubertin, who was to retire the following year. They also gave France a chance to redeem its international reputation after the unsatisfactory 1900 Games. The number of competitors in 1924 topped 3000 for the first time – although there were only 136 women. The performances of Harold Abrahams in the men's 100m and of Eric Liddell in the 400m were subsequently immortalised in the 1981 film *Chariots of Fire*.

The year 1924 also saw the first independent Winter Olympics – also held in France. They continued to take place in the same year as the Summer Games until 1992, when it was decided that future Winter Olympic Games would take place two years after (or before) the Summer Games. It was also in 1924 that the Olympic motto – Citius, Altius, Fortius (Swifter, Higher, Stronger) – was first used.

There were some problems in the 1924 Games, though, attributed to the fanaticism of the Parisian spectators. Ill-feeling was particularly strong between the French and Americans, and during one rugby match between France and the USA, an American spectator was beaten up by a French one. After the 1924 Games some newspapers called for them to be abolished, but this view did not prevail.

Amsterdam 1928

The 1928 Games proved to be very open, with competitors from 28 different nations winning gold medals.

Women competed in track and field and gymnastics for the first time, although some anti-feminists argued that some events were too dangerous for women. Asian athletes won their first-ever gold medals, while India won the hockey, a feat they would repeat every time through to the 1960 Games in Rome.

It was in Amsterdam that the Olympic flame first burned in the stadium and doves were released at the opening ceremony for the first time.

Los Angeles 1932

The Los Angeles Games in 1932 were held in the middle of the Great Depression of the 1930s, and for the first time they were compressed into a two-week period. The economic climate resulted in only 1400 competitors taking part, which meant that participation was the lowest since 1906. Only three countries entered the hockey, and the football competition had to be dropped. Not surprisingly, the USA dominated proceedings, winning, for example, all 12 diving gold medals.

However, the Games were deemed successful, with 18 world records broken or tied, and record numbers of spectators in attendance. They were held in the period of 'prohibition', but the USA lifted its ban on alcohol to allow some of the teams to import and drink wine. (The French team claimed that wine was an essential part of their diet.)

It was also in 1932 that the photo-finish made its Olympic debut.

Berlin 1936

Berlin saw a Games with over 4000 participants from 49 countries, and these Games are remembered for Hitler's attempt to use them for propaganda purposes and for Jesse Owens's fabulous contribution on the track. When the decision was taken in 1931 that Berlin be awarded the 1936 Games, few could have foreseen the rise of Hitler and Nazism and, as 1936 approached, some countries called for a boycott. An alternative Games was planned for Spain, but was, ironically, cancelled because of the outbreak of the Spanish Civil War.

The black American Jesse Owens won the 100m, 200m, long jump and sprint relay and, despite the growing strength of the Nazi state, the German people took him to their hearts – so much so that a street in Berlin would be named in his honour after his death in 1980.

The 1936 Games were broadcast on television for the first time – although only within Berlin, where 25 large television screens were set up in theatres around the city, allowing people to see the Games free of charge. These Games also saw a new Olympic motto: 'The most important thing in the Olympic

Games is not to win but to take part, just as the most important thing in life is not the triumph but the struggle. The essential thing is not to have conquered, but to have fought well.' The Games of 1936 also introduced the Olympic torch relay.

The Olympics and the year 1940

The Summer and Winter Games were awarded to Japan, but when this country invaded China, it lost them. The Winter Games were then re-scheduled for Germany, only to have that cancelled when Germany invaded Poland. The Summer Games were next awarded to Helsinki, but when Russia invaded Poland, they were, like the Winter Games, cancelled altogether.

As the Second World War was still in progress, no Games were scheduled for 1944.

London 1948

The Olympics resumed in 1948, after a gap of 12 years as a result of the Second World War. There were 50 countries represented, but Germany and Japan were banned because of their participation in the war. London was chosen – like Antwerp in 1920 – in recognition of the damage the city had suffered in the war. For the first time, the action was widely viewed on televisions in people's homes.

Audrey Patterson became the first black woman to win a medal when she took bronze in the 200m, while two people, Ilona Elek and Jan Brzak, successfully defended titles from the 1936 Games. Fanny Blankers-Koen won four events, the 100m, 80m hurdles, 200m and sprint relay, having entered the Games as a world record holder in six events.

Helsinki 1952

The Helsinki Olympics belonged to the Zatopek family, and more especially Emile. Wife Dana won the javelin, but Emile entered history with a long-distance treble. Having won the 10,000m in 1948, he repeated the feat in Helsinki and then won the 5000m three days later. To cap it all, he then won the marathon and is still the only man in Olympic history ever to win all three at the same Games. The Soviet Union entered a team for the first time, and dominated the gymnastics; West Germany also competed for the first time; and Taiwan withdrew as a protest over the acceptance of the People's Republic of China. The number of athletes stayed at just over 4000, but the number of countries had grown to 69.

Melbourne 1956

The number of participants at this Games dropped to 3184 from 67 countries, including several new countries, as the Olympics were hit by two boycotts – Egypt, Iraq and Lebanon were absent in protest at the Israeli–led invasion of the Suez Canal, while Holland, Spain and Switzerland refused to participate after the Russian invasion of Hungary, just one month earlier.

Ironically, a Hungarian, Laszlo Papp, became the first boxer to win three gold medals. When Hungary met Russia in water polo, tensions boiled over and the game was stopped after a brawl occurred. Hungary won the match 4–0, and ultimately the gold medal.

This was the first-ever Olympics in the Southern Hemisphere and the latest in the calendar year – the Summer Games ended on 8 December.

Equestrian events were held in Sweden, as Australian quarantine regulations were so strict that the entry of foreign horses into the country was too difficult. At the end of the Games, athletes marched together – not by individual nations – as a symbol of their unity.

Rome 1960

After the volcanic activity robbed them of the Games in 1908, Italy waited 52 years for another opportunity. In 1960, participants exceeded 5000, with 83 countries involved. Ghanaian boxer Ike Quartey became the first-ever black African medallist in the Olympics by winning a silver medal; and five days later Abebe Bikila of Ethiopia won black Africa's first gold, in the marathon. Sante Gaiardoni of Italy pleased the home crowd when he became the first man in Olympic history to win both cycling's time trial and the match sprint events.

The year 1960 saw the first global television broadcast of the Games and, at the other end of the historical spectrum, the wrestling bouts took place on a site where the ancient Romans had held their wrestling competitions.

The gold medal in boxing's light-heavyweight division went to an 18-year-old American, Cassius Marcellus Clay, later to become World Champion as Muhammad Ali.

Tokyo 1964

The first Games to be held in Asia saw South Africa banned for apartheid and another batch of world records set in the swimming events. World records were broken in eight of the 10 men's pool events, with American Don Schollander taking four golds, and Dawn Fraser winning the 100m freestyle for the third time. Larysa Latynina of Ukraine joined the select band of people to win nine gold medals.

Mexico City 1968

These Games were held at altitude (7347 feet), a fact that disadvantaged the long-distance runners but gave sprinters and jumpers a huge advantage. New world records were set in all men's sprint events of 400m or shorter, while five different athletes broke the record in the triple jump. The Games also gave a significant advantage to athletes who lived or trained at high altitude and therefore were used to this environment.

Lee Evans's time of 43.86 for the 400m would stand for 29 years, while Bob Beamon will be remembered for ever for his spectacular long jump of 8.90 metres, a mark that would only be broken 23 years later. On the other hand, the winning times in the 5000m and 10,000m were the slowest for 16 and 20 years respectively.

For the first time, over 100 countries were involved. On a sad note, though, the Games saw the first drug disqualification, as modern pentathlete Hans-Gunnar Liljenwall tested positive, and was disqualified, for excessive alcohol. (In 1967 the IOC had taken the pioneering step of establishing a medical commission.)

The Games ended on a controversial note when American athletes Tommie Smith and John Carlos were removed from the Olympic Village by the IOC. In protest at the Mexican government's killing of at least 250 unarmed demonstrators on the eve of the Games, the two men staged a silent Black Power protest with a raised fist salute, during the 200m award ceremony. It didn't go down well with the IOC, who promptly ordered the USA to send them home.

Peter Norman, the Australian silver medallist in the 200m, wore a civil rights badge on the podium in opposition to his country's White Australia immigration policy.

Munich 1972

The largest Olympics to date, with 121 nations bringing more than 7000 athletes, is sadly remembered more for the killing of 11 Israeli competitors by eight Palestinian terrorists, than for the sports competition itself. After a 34-hour pause, during which time a memorial service was held, the Games resumed.

Although the remaining events were overshadowed by the

tragic deaths, there were still some top performances. Mark Spitz was the most successful competitor, winning seven golds in the pool to take his overall Olympic total to nine, while Olga Korbut became a world star in the gymnastics, failing to take the individual gold but rallying to win team and apparatus golds.

Montreal 1976

The 1976 Games almost crippled Montreal and Canada financially, but were a success in sporting terms, although 22 African nations boycotted them over the apartheid issue.

The undoubted star of the Games was 14-year-old Romanian Nadia Comeneci, who stunned the world by scoring the first-ever perfect 10 on the asymmetrical bars and the beam, and going on to score seven perfect 10s in all.

The pool saw more world records set than any other discipline, as records were set in 21 of the 26 events, while another record was matched. East German women won 11 of their 13 events, having not won a single gold four years before. How the East Germans made such rapid progress in four years can only be a matter of conjecture.

The Soviet Union and East Germany finished way ahead of the rest in the overall medals table and, at the other end of the scale, Clarence Hill won Bermuda's first-ever medal — a bronze in boxing's super-heavyweight division. Bermuda is the smallest island ever to win a medal.

Moscow 1980

With the Soviet invasion of Afghanistan in the previous year still uppermost in the minds of the Western world, American President Jimmy Carter ordered a boycott of the Games by the US team. Other countries, including Canada, West Germany, Japan, Kenya and China, were also absent, leaving the Games with just 5200 participants from 80 countries; and some of the participants in the Games boycotted the opening ceremony.

Despite this, it was a great sporting event, and more world records were broken than in Montreal. Not surprisingly, the Soviet and East German teams once again dominated most of the events, particularly on the track. Incredibly, every one of the 54 East German rowers participating won a medal, while East German women again won 11 of the 13 events in the pool, and Russian gymnast Nicolai Andrianov was the most successful athlete of the Games, taking five golds to take his Olympic total to 15.

Women's hockey was held for the first time, but the boycott resulted in five of the original six entrants not taking part. Zimbabwe was invited to be a replacement just five weeks before the Games. Their team was selected just one week before and, with minimal preparation, won gold!

Los Angeles 1984

The Summer Games returned to the USA for the first time since the Second World War, and to Los Angeles for the second time. However, the Games suffered from counter-boycotts, with almost all the communist world boycotting the Games in retaliation for the USA's refusal to take part in Moscow four years previously.

In the absence of the awesome Eastern European track team, the Americans were, predictably, the biggest beneficiaries. Carl Lewis emulated the great Jesse Owens, 48 years before, to win the 100m, 200m, long jump and sprint relay, and was the true track star of the Games. France won the first football tournament where professionals were allowed to compete.

The Games made a profit of 215 million dollars and are seen as the origin of modern corporate sponsorship. In 1976 some 600 companies had had an involvement, but by 1984 the number had been reduced to about 70 in three categories – official sponsor, supplier and licensee.

Seoul 1988

Despite the tension between the two Koreas, the Olympic truce was respected and Russia and East Germany, traditional power-houses, returned to the fold after their boycott of Los Angeles four years earlier. A total of 8465 athletes from 159 countries took part, with 237 events in 23 sports.

A hard track made the Games perfect for sprinting, and it was reflected in both the men's and women's sprints as both world records were smashed. Ben Johnson's awesome run of 9.79 to beat Carl Lewis did not stand, as Johnson was found guilty of taking steroids. He thus became the first big-name athlete to test positive for drugs.

The scandal rocked the Games and cast doubt on the truly outstanding performances of Florence Griffith Joyner. This American, who had won silver at 400m in 1984, broke the world records beyond all recognition in the 100m and 200m finals. Her time of 10.49 would have given her seventh place in the men's final, and though she would 'retire' under a cloud not long after the Olympics, her times remain a reminder of the most incredible sprinting ever achieved by a woman.

Matt Biondi and Janet Evans were the American stars in the pool, winning eight golds between them; and tennis returned to the Games for the first time in 64 years, with Steffi Graf winning the women's title, and Miloslav Mecir the men's.

Barcelona 1992

For the first time in 20 years, all nations were represented as the new world order took over. South Africa, having abolished apartheid, competed as Olympic unity was restored after the spate of boycotts in previous Games. There were 9364 partici-pants from 169 countries.

Barcelona was an inspired choice for the Games of the twenty-fifth Olympiad. It is a vibrant and colourful city, with spectacular architecture and the famous Ramblas promenade running down from the heart of the city to the port, which bustles with boats large and small. Towering over the port is Montjuic, at the top of which stands the Olympic stadium. The steep climb up Montjuic each morning was made easier by the escalators – a luxury denied the marathon runners – and the slow descent after the day's competition was enlivened by the dancing fountains accompanied by a fantastic music and light show.

Inside the stadium, the atmosphere was tremendous – even though the Spaniards had a habit of whistling and jeering false starts, and gave Khalid Skah the rudest of responses after that controversial 10,000m in which he and his fellow Moroccan Boutayeb seemed to run as a team to thwart the Kenyan Chelimo. Skah was disqualified but reinstated on appeal. The Games, though, were full of incident and accident – with Gail Devers falling over the last barrier when leading the 100m hurdles; Carl Lewis's revenge in the long jump; the gold medals of Linford Christie and Sally Gunnell; and the downfall of the three hottest favourites, Messrs Morcelli, Johnson and Bubka.

Linford Christie became, at 32, the oldest ever winner as he raced to a superb victory over a host of top Americans. Carl Lewis, who hadn't made the US team in the sprints (just a year after setting a world record in the 100m), gained consolation by anchoring the sprint relay team to victory and won his eighth Olympic gold with a third long jump win in consecutive Olympics – which he was to make four in a row in 1996.

There were two dramatic finishes. Spain won the football final, scoring with just 72 seconds left to play. In the water-polo final it took six periods of overtime for Italy to beat Spain.

Atlanta 1996

Atlanta pipped Athens for the right to host the centenary Games and they proved a success, at least on the sporting field, with over 10,000 participants from 197 countries.

However, the Games were hit by organisational problems and then a bomb was set off in the Olympic Park, killing one person and injuring more than 100. The Games went ahead, though, and as always there were some outstanding performances both on the track and outside. The USA took the medal glory with 44 golds, and it was one of the best American athletes of all time, Carl Lewis, who carved himself another niche in history. His leap of 8.50 metres won the long jump gold and made him one of only three Olympians to win a total of nine golds.

The problems with drugs continued to blight the spirit of the Olympics as Michelle Smith stunned the world with three golds in the pool, causing her rivals to accuse her of taking illegal substances. She tested negative, but was later banned for refusing to take a test.

Sydney 2000

Sydney 2000 was a wonderful Olympics. Who can forget the night Australia stopped to watch as Cathy Freeman took the 400m for the host country, or the women's water polo when the Aussies scored the winning goal, in literally the last seconds?

The atmosphere in the city was electric. For those who couldn't get tickets, there were many other places around the city where big screens were set up for the crowds of people to watch the events in a great atmosphere.

Athens 2004

And so the wheel has come full circle as the 2004 Olympic Games return to their original venue in Greece. A magnificent experience is in store.

2

Memorable
Olympic Moments

Seoul 1988 – men's 100m

The final of the men's 100m in the 1988 Olympics was an eagerly awaited race. However, it proved to be an infamous race that is still vividly remembered and talked about. In 1984 Carl Lewis had won the 100m in 9.99, and Ben Johnson had taken the bronze in 10.22.

In 1985 Johnson defeated Carl Lewis for the first time – after losing to him in seven consecutive races. Ironically, he was quoted as saying, 'I want to be the best on my own natural ability and no drugs will pass into my body.' In 1987 Johnson won the World Championship in a time of 9.83; this was no surprise as he had beaten Lewis in their last four meetings.

The Olympic 100m race of 1988 was billed as a great duel between the two men. Lewis was the reigning Olympic champion, and Johnson the World Champion and the world record holder. However, in reality it was a one-sided duel, as Johnson was far ahead of Lewis and was proving it regularly.

The year 1988 turned out to be a wretched one for Johnson. He suffered a hamstring injury in February, and recovered only to aggravate it in May. The September Olympics were getting closer. When Carl Lewis ran 9.99 in June he could fairly state, 'I am running better than ever and Ben isn't running at all.'

In August the pair met in Rome. Lewis won in 9.93, with Johnson third. With characteristic modesty, Lewis said, 'The gold medal is mine. I will never again lose to Johnson.'

By the time the Olympic final came round, it was a more even prospect. During the previous two years, Johnson had the edge, but current form favoured Lewis. The final was scheduled scarcely 90 minutes after the semi-finals – Lewis won one semi in 9.97, Johnson the other in 10.03.

The race was a thrilling piece of sport. Some Olympic events last for hours, so one mistake is not important – there is time to make up for it. The 100m is different as it is over in just 10 seconds. There is no second chance; a slow start, a slight stumble, and the race is gone. The tension before the start was almost unbearable. There was some wind, but it was within the legal limit. Any world record would stand.

Carl Lewis, the defending champion, undefeated in 1988, liked to be the last to settle into his blocks. He liked to make the others wait, to unsettle them.

This time, though, Johnson 'out-Lewises' him, and Johnson is the last to the blocks. Last into the blocks and first out of them. He reacts in 0.132 to Lewis's 0.136. Johnson is increasing his lead. Johnson reaches 60 metres in 6.37; Lewis in 6.51. Johnson is travelling at 26.95 m.p.h. At 80 metres, Johnson is 0.17 ahead. For the first time in the race Lewis is running faster. Some 5 metres short of the line, Johnson puts his arm in the air to celebrate his victory.

Johnson won! He broke the world record. Calvin Smith ran a brilliant 9.99, but finished out of the medals. It was simply the fastest anyone had ever run; 47 strides had taken Johnson from the gun to the tape. The results were:

Ben Johnson	9.79
Carl Lewis	9.92
Linford Christie	9.97
Calvin Smith	9.99

In another of those great ironies, when Johnson was later asked which meant more to him, the world record or the gold medal, he replied, 'The medal. It is something that no one can take away from you.'

After the race, Johnson was asked for a urine sample, which was then analysed in the IOC-accredited laboratory in Seoul. Following standard procedure, the sample was divided into two – the A and B. The A was analysed and the B was retained. A large number of samples were tested during the Games, all identified anonymously with a code number. The laboratory provided results by code number – therefore having no idea whose sample was being tested.

The director of the laboratory, Dr Jongsei Park, informed the IOC chairman of the medical commission, Prince Alexandre de Merode, that sample number xxx had tested positive. The race was in the early afternoon of Saturday 24 September, and Prince Alexandre was informed of the result at 23.00 hours on 25 September. The chairman then retrieved the list of codes, linking athletes to samples, from his safe. It is hard to imagine Prince Alexandre's reaction when he saw the name of Ben Johnson, the winner of the highest-profile event in the Games, staring up at him.

He then wrote a letter to the Canadian chef de mission, Carol Anne Letheren, and she was awakened to receive it at 1.45 a.m. on Monday 26 September. By 7.00 a.m. she had consulted the Canadian chief medical officer and others in the team, including Johnson's coach and physician. Three members of the delegation exercised their right to be present at the examination of the B sample. This also was positive. Both samples contained 90 nanograms of an anabolic steroid called stanozolol.

Further meetings took place and, as the Canadian delegation could offer no explanation of the test result, Johnson was stripped of his medal; and by Tuesday morning (27 September), three days after the final, he was on his way home, a disgraced athlete.

Ben Johnson was born in Jamaica in 1961, but at the age of 15 he emigrated with his family to Canada. The following year he met Charlie Francis, a former world-class sprinter, who became his coach, staying with him throughout his career.

In 1982 Johnson won silver at the Commonwealth Games, in 1984 the Olympic bronze, and in 1986 the Commonwealth gold, before becoming world champion in 1987. At some point along the line, Francis suggested to Johnson that he take steroids to improve his performance; Francis is said to have told him that steroids could give him a metre's advantage – ironically, the distance by which he defeated Lewis in 1988. Looked at from another point of view, if Johnson could beat Lewis by a metre with the aid of the drug, one wonders whether he could have sneaked a victory without?

Fifteen years on, the race is still remembered, and *The Times* ran a series of articles in September 2002 to mark the fifteenth anniversary of this race. Johnson himself recently revisited Seoul for the first time since 1988 to make a television documentary about the events. Much has been written about the race in the intervening period, and some things are clearer, but others are more mysterious than ever.

At the time, the received wisdom was that Johnson had cheated to gain an edge over seven clean and innocent athletes in that final. With hindsight, that may not be an entirely accurate picture. There is no evidence that any of the others was benefiting from an illegal substance in 1988, but Dennis Mitchell and Linford Christie subsequently tested positive. Carl Lewis was never found guilty, but there have been persistent rumours of positive tests being hushed up.

In fact, Linford Christie tested positive in the 200m at Seoul, but claimed that the cause was ginseng tea and the IOC gave him 'the benefit of the doubt'. Ben Johnson was to say later, 'Linford got away with it in 1988. Why should Ben Johnson pay the price for everyone else doing the same thing? The only way they could get rid of Ben Johnson was to come up with an excuse like a banned substance I have never used in my life.'

Calvin Smith, who finished fourth, told *The Times* that he was arguably the real winner because of the subsequent doubt about the three who beat him. He said, 'Throughout the last five or ten years of my career, I knew I was being denied the chance to show that I was the best clean runner. I knew I was competing against athletes who were on drugs.' Ray Stewart, who finished eighth in the final, also expressed the view that drug-taking was rife in 1988 and that fingers pointing at Johnson were just as dirty as Ben himself.

Having denied any involvement with drugs at the time, Johnson and his advisers have subsequently admitted that he had used steroids since 1981. Charlie Francis, Johnson's coach, stated that Ben was on a drugs programme, but vehemently denied that he was on the type or quantity of drug for which he tested positive. Francis added, 'Everyone broke the rules, why pick on one or two?'

However, this admission raised as many questions as it answered, questions like these:

1 Knowing that if he won a medal he was likely to be tested, why would Johnson have taken a drug immediately before the final? (Johnson's camp later said that he had taken his last drug 26 days before the race — to ensure that all traces were out of his system.)
2 If he was going to take a drug, why stanozolol, which would not have enhanced his performance? (Johnson's camp said he was taking furazobol, not stanozolol.)

Several theories have been put forward to explain the positive test:

1 Johnson panicked before the race and took stanozolol from his own private supply of drugs, believing it would help him.

2 Francis, and Johnson's other advisers, are not telling the truth.

3 Sabotage – someone spiked his drink or his sample.

4 The sample that tested positive was not Johnson's.

Owen Slot and John Goodbody concluded their *Times'* investigations with, 'That Johnson cheated is beyond doubt. We have his own word on that. But how and why he was caught, we may never know.'

Moscow 1980 – men's 800m and 1500m

The year 1980 found British middle-distance running on the crest of a wave, with Seb Coe and Steve Ovett the top two in the world in their events. The anticipated head-to-head battles between the two in the 800m and 1500m were the most eagerly anticipated races of the Olympic Games.

The pair's dominance of the events was total. Leading up to the 1980 Olympics, Ovett had not been beaten over 1500m and the mile for 42 races. In 1979 Coe had broken the 800m, 1500m and mile world records inside a groundbreaking 41 days. That the two rivals had not raced against each other for two years only added to the aura surrounding the Moscow clashes. The outcome was both expected and unexpected, as Coe and Ovett each won gold. The surprise element was that each won his supposed weaker event.

The first event was the 800m. Coe recognises that he was the favourite: 'I was, by some distance, the fastest on paper over 800, but the Olympic Games is historically one of the most brutal disregarders of current form and status.'

In a slow 800m final it was Ovett who took gold. He was in sixth place after one lap, but fought through the crowd to be second on the final bend. With 70 metres left, he shot past Coe to win by three metres. Coe, who had left the final charge too late after struggling to read the race, was left to reflect on a personal tactical nightmare: 'I have always said that if you wanted to commit every cardinal sin that it was possible to commit at 800m inside a minute-and-three-quarters, that's the video to watch,' said Coe, who had to settle for silver.

Having won the 800m and with his stronger event still to come, Ovett was odds-on favourite to complete the double – but it was not to be. Afterwards, Seb Coe admitted that it had taken a lot of effort to pick himself up after the disappointment of his failure to win the 800m. It helped, though, that he had the opportunity to get back on the track quickly. Coe recalls telling himself on the eve of the 1500m that 'there are no tomorrows'. It was all or nothing on the day. On the final curve, Coe kicked into the lead and held off the challenge of Ovett and surprise silver medallist Jurgen Straub. He said afterwards, 'It was complete relief that you've got there and you are going to go away from the Games with a gold medal.'

Four years later in Los Angeles, Coe became the first man successfully to defend his 1500m crown. In contrast, Ovett had a wretched time in 1984. Suffering from bronchitis, he barely made the final. He finished eighth, but collapsed and spent two nights in hospital. Showing great courage, he ran in the 1500m, reached the final, and was in contention on the final lap before collapsing with chest pains.

By the time he retired, Coe had four Olympic medals and 12 world records to show for his athletics career. But his career came to a sad end when, as reigning Olympic 1500m champion (1980 and 1984), he failed to gain selection for the British team for the 1988 Olympics.

Los Angeles 1984 – women's 3000m

The 3000m for women has only been held three times in the Olympics – 1984, 1988 and 1992. The first-ever women's Olympic 3000m was won by Maricica Puica of Romania from

Wendy Sly of Great Britain, with Lynn Williams of Canada taking bronze. However, the sad fact is that no one remembers any of them. The race is better remembered for an incident between Zola Budd and Mary Decker.

Mary Decker was a champion middle-distance runner, stunning track fans and competitors alike with her seemingly effortless, long, loping strides, strong finishes, and tenacious determination. In 1982 she broke seven world and US records, at distances ranging from 800m to 10,000m. Unbeaten in the period 1980–3, at one time she held the US records for the mile and for the 800m, 1500m, 3000m, 5000m and 10,000m. She completed the 1500m and 3000m double at the 1983 World Championships.

The only thing missing from Decker's repertoire was an Olympic medal – in fact, she hadn't even run in an Olympic race. In 1972 she was too young, being only 14; in 1976 she was injured; and in 1980 the USA boycotted the Moscow Olympics. With the 1984 Olympics in her home country – and in Los Angeles, the city where she'd grown up – she was a strong favourite. At 26, she was in her prime.

Zola Budd grew up in South Africa under the rule of apartheid, and South Africa was, at that stage, in the middle of the period of banishment from the Olympics (1960–92). As a barefoot teenager, Zola Budd started breaking records when she was 13. In January 1984 she ran 5000m in 15:1.83 – seven seconds faster than Mary Decker's existing world record. However, as South Africa was excluded from world athletics, the time could not be recognised as a world record.

Determined to compete at the 1984 Olympics, Budd applied for British citizenship on the grounds that she had a British grandfather. Amid controversy, she was fast-tracked through the system and awarded a passport in time to run for Britain in the Olympics.

Budd and Decker eased into the final, with Decker the more impressive of the two. Her semi-final win in 8:44.38 had been, as she put it, 'Effortless – except for Lynn Williams [of Canada] stepping on my heel four times.' She said she was looking for about an 8:29 pace in the final. Budd was not a renowned fast-finisher; she wanted a fast race.

One incident lightened the tension for Budd on the day of the Olympic final. The athletes in the 3000m final had to show their running spikes to an official, whose task it was to see that the spikes conformed to specifications. Zola recalls, 'I was barefoot, so I just picked up my feet and showed them to him, white plasters on my toes and all. The poor man nearly cracked up laughing, but what else could I have done? Everybody else had spikes and I had to show him something.'

The race began. At halfway, the main contenders looked good. Decker's tactics were to step up the pace with 1000 metres to go, in order to neutralise Puica's fast finish. So far so good. Budd was outside Decker's right shoulder – where she had been almost from the start. They had bumped elbows at 500 metres, a result of Budd's wide-swinging arm action, and Decker had shot her a sharp look.

At about 1600 metres, Budd started to make her presence felt. As Decker said later, 'She was cutting in on the turn, without being near passing.' Kenny Moore, of *Sports Illustrated* magazine, describes what happened next:

By the end of the turn, Budd appeared to have enough margin to cut in without interfering with Decker's stride, but instead she hung wide, on the outside of Lane 1, as they came into the stretch. Decker was near the rail, a yard behind Budd. Budd's team-mate, Wendy Sly, had come up to third, off Budd's shoulder, and Puica was fourth, tucked in tight behind Decker, waiting.

Decker sensed Budd drifting to the inside. 'She tried to cut in without being, basically, ahead,' Decker would say. But Decker didn't do what a seasoned middle-distance runner would have done. She didn't reach out to Budd's shoulder to let her know she was there, too close behind for Budd to move to the pole. Instead, Decker shortened her stride for a couple of steps. There was contact. Decker's right thigh grazed Budd's left foot. Budd took five more strides, slightly off balance. Trying to regain control, she swayed in slightly to the left. Decker's right foot struck Budd's left calf, low, just above the Achilles tendon. Budd's left leg shot out, and she was near falling.

But Decker was falling, tripped by that leg all askew. 'To keep from pushing her, I fell,' she would say. She reached out after Budd, inadvertently tearing the number from her back and went headlong across the rail on to the infield.

Decker's competitiveness is without limit. 'My first thought was, "I have to get up",' she said. But when she tried, 'It felt like I was tied to the ground.' She had a pulled gluteus, the hip stabiliser muscle. Only then, understanding that she couldn't go on, with the field past and the medical attendants and her fiancé, Richard Slaney, running across the track to her, did the anguish come. Hers was the horrible realisation that once again, in the race she'd been denied by injury and boycott for eight years, she was being denied any chance of a conclusion of her own making.

Budd was booed and jeered by the American crowd for the rest of the race and finished seventh. After the event, Budd went to apologise but Decker dismissed her, saying, 'Don't bother!' – leaving Zola in tears. Budd was then disqualified but later reinstated, and the incident was regarded as an unfortunate accident.

Budd continued her career after the Olympics, setting a world record for the 5000m in 1985 and an indoor world 3000m record in 1986. She was banned from the Commonwealth Games in 1986 and returned to South Africa. Budd competed in the 1992 Olympics, but without success.

Mary Decker (now Slaney) competed in the 1988 and 1996

Olympics, but finished her career without an Olympic medal. In 1996 she was given a two-year ban for a drugs offence.

That race in 1984 was a sad occasion, from which neither girl ever fully recovered.

Mexico City 1968 – men's long jump

The 1968 long jump had several potential winners. Lynn Davies, the reigning Olympic champion, was there to defend his title, and so were the joint world record holders, Igor Terovanesyan of the USSR, and Ralph Boston of the USA. Then there was the American Bob Beamon.

The competition started. Boston broke the Olympic record with 8.33 – close to the world record of 8.35. Beamon had two no-jumps and a safe jump of 8.19. Then there was a break for lunch.

Soon it was Beamon's turn again. This time he soared through the air and landed – it was big! In fact, it was too big for the officials. He had jumped beyond the scope of the officials' measuring device! When it was measured and double-checked, it came to 8.90 metres. His first words were, apparently, 'Tell me I am not dreaming.' Later, as he reflected, he was still in shock. 'I was not anticipating anything other than winning the gold medal. I can't explain it. I just made a fantastic leap.'

Afterwards, Soviet competitor Igor Terovanesyan said, 'Compared to this jump, we are as children.' English jumper Lynn Davies said to Beamon angrily, 'You have destroyed this event!'

Surprisingly, this record did not stand for ever, as Mike Powell jumped 8.95 in the 1991 World Championships.

Barcelona 1992 – men's 400m

The scene is the 1992 Olympic Games, and the semi-final of the men's 400m. Derek Redmond, the British record holder, is running. Redmond had had to pull out of the 1988 Olympics at the last minute with an injury, and the next four years had seen him enduring a succession of operations, mainly for Achilles tendon problems. In the 1991 World Championships he made no impact on the individual race, but was in the historic UK 4×400m relay team, which won the gold.

Now at last it was beginning to happen for Redmond, and in the heat in Barcelona he was flying. In the semi-final he started well, but then after 150 metres he pulled up sharply, clutching his hamstring. The Olympic dream was over, and minutes later he was weeping inconsolably on the trackside.

Then he picked himself up and started limping round the track – and somehow his father got through security and on to the track. Redmond put an arm on his father's shoulder and together they slowly made the finishing line. A personal tragedy, but the way Redmond handled it made it an unforgettable Olympic moment.

Roll of dishonour

There have been many Olympic heroes, but there have also been a few villains along the way. In the ancient Games, each competitor had to take an oath to compete according to the rules, and the organisers devised an excellent way of dealing with cheats: they were fined. The sting in the tail was that the fine was used to commission a statue of the cheat, which was displayed, with an inscription of his name, father's name and city. It was a veritable roll of dishonour. Even the Apostle Paul was aware of the practice, when he wrote to Timothy, 'If anyone competes as an athlete, he does not receive the victor's crown unless he competes according to the rules' (2 Timothy 2:5).

In the 1904 marathon, Fred Lorz was the first to cross the line, but it was then discovered that he had stopped running after nine miles, and then taken a car ride for 11 miles before resuming running for the remaining distance. Consequently, Thomas Hicks was declared the real winner of the race.

In 1976 Boris Onyshchenko, a Russian pentathlete, managed to wire up his fencing equipment so that he appeared to be scoring points when he wasn't. He was eventually rumbled and sent home in disgrace.

The 20-kilometre race-walker, Jane Saville, was disqualified while only 100 metres (and leading the race) from the finish – her tear-filled face was one of the haunting images of Sydney 2000.

Honourable moments

On a far more positive note, there have also been some amazing examples of sportsmanship. In 1908, Sweden's Mauritz Andersson agreed to the postponement of the middleweight Greco-Roman wrestling final to allow his opponent Frithiof Martensson to recover from an injury. Martensson recovered so well that he won!

In 1964 the British two-man bob (bobsleigh) team of Robin Dixon and Tony Nash were in contention for the gold medal. After the first of their two runs, the British pair discovered that the main bolt holding their back axle in place had snapped in half, and there would be no time to have a replacement brought out.

The British pair's main rival, current world champion Eugenio Monte of Italy, hearing of the Britons' plight, removed the bolt from his own bob after his second run, to have it fitted in the British bob. The Britons then won the gold medal. As Robin Dixon of the British team pointed out, 'Monte knew that he was sacrificing his chance of an Olympic gold medal, the only significant prize that he had not won, by his action.'

Monte's own comment on the incident was, 'My action was very normal for a sportsperson. You try to help the other people to have the same conditions that you have.' Eugenio still has the mug presented to him by the British team, with its inscription: 'A great sporting gesture'. Monte clearly embodied the Olympic spirit and ideals.

3

Eric Liddell, the Flying Scotsman

It is 80 years since Eric Liddell competed in the Olympics for the only time, and yet his name is still very familiar to us. Can you name one other competitor who competed in the Olympics of 1924? Probably not. So what is the abiding attraction of, and fascination with, Eric Liddell?

The 1981 film *Chariots of Fire* certainly raised Eric's profile and brought the story to a wide audience. But that begs, as much as answers, the question, 'Why should a commercial film-maker have regarded an event at the 1924 Olympics to be worthy of a film in the 1980s?'

The story of Eric Liddell had already been documented in a booklet, and a book, by Eric's contemporary, D. P. Thompson. Since then, there have been at least seven books and two television programmes on Eric. He was, by all accounts, one of the most saintly men who ever lived. A typical tribute to him at his funeral or memorial service was, 'Yesterday a man said to me, "Of all men I have known, Eric Liddell was the one in whose character and life the spirit of Jesus Christ was pre-eminently manifested." '

Eric Henry Liddell was born on 16 January 1902 in Tientsin, Northern China, of missionary parents. He was intended to be Henry Eric Liddell until someone pointed out that the initials 'HEL' might be inappropriate for a missionary's child! At the age of five he saw Scotland for the first time, and from 1908 to 1920 he was educated at the School for the Sons of Missionaries (Eltham College) in south-east London, along with his elder brother, Rob.

Without the modern communications that we now take for granted, missionary service was much more complicated and demanding in those days. For missionaries and their families, separation was a way of life. When six-year-old Eric said goodbye to his father in 1908 – Eric staying at school and his father returning to China – he would not see him again for 13 years. He was also separated from his mother for 11 of those 13 years.

Eric's comment on school to his sister Jenny summed up his priorities, 'I don't think much of the lessons, but I can run.' In fact, he excelled at athletics and rugby, while also doing enough to pass his exams. At the University of Edinburgh (1920–4) he took a science degree, won seven caps for Scotland at rugby, and established himself as a runner.

After competing in the 1924 Olympics, Eric set off for China where he served with the London Missionary Society, initially as a teacher and subsequently as a travelling evangelist. He remained in China, apart from two periods of furlough, until his death in 1945 in a (Japanese) internment camp in Weihsien, China.

However, to return to university: Eric was initially a reluctant runner, and when first asked to run in the university sports, he declined, saying that he was too busy. Eventually he was persuaded to take part, which he did successfully, whereupon, having won the first event he entered, he just carried on running and winning.

By 1923 there was speculation about whether he would make the Olympic team for Paris 1924. For today's British athlete there are two World Championships, a European Championship, the Commonwealth Games and four European Cups to fit into the four years between Olympics. In Liddell's day none of these existed. The Olympics were the only international championships.

July 1923 effectively settled the issue of Olympic selection. On 6–7 July, Eric went to London to compete in the AAAs championship. He won both the 100 yards – in 9.7, a time that remained the UK record until 1958 – and the 220 yards. The following weekend he took part in three races – 100 yards, 220 yards and 440 yards in a Triangular International at Stoke on Trent, and won all three.

However, it is the 440 event that is remembered. At that time, the 400/440 was not usually run in lanes and, about three strides into the race, another runner cut across Eric, tripped him, and left him lying on the ground. He got up again and set off after the other runners who were now well ahead of him, and continued running until he overtook all the others and won the event! Reporting on the race, one newspaper remarked, 'The circumstances in which he won made it a performance bordering on the miraculous.'

When it emerged that the heats of the Olympic 100m were to take place on a Sunday, he declined to run, entering instead the 200m and 400m. At this point we need to separate fact from fiction. *Chariots of Fire* portrays Eric on his way to Paris for the Olympics, discovering that the 100m heats were on a Sunday and deciding not to compete. The myth goes further, in that the film portrays Eric as choosing to run only the 400m, a distance he had never run before! In reality, he had several months of preparation for the 200m and 400m.

In fact, he knew the schedule several months earlier – possibly in late 1923. Eric had a strong principle of observing Sunday and not running on this day. He didn't make a fuss, though. He just said quietly, but firmly, 'I'm not running'.

It has to be noted, too, that attitudes to Sunday were significantly different in the 1920s compared with now, as was the amount of competition that took place on Sundays. The practice of honouring the Sabbath by refusing to compete on the Lord's Day was a normal attitude at that time – in the 1900 Olympics in Paris, a number of athletes did not compete when their events were scheduled for Sunday. In fact, prior to the 1924 Games, the British Olympic Association Council sought a change to the dates of the 100m race, requesting that 'athletes who object to running or taking part in any game on a Sunday, be given a chance to have their race or event arranged on another day'.

As well as the 100m, Eric also sacrificed a place in the 4×100m and the 4×400m relays as those finals were also to be run on the final Sunday of the Games.

With hindsight, we might ask why it is that athletes who achieved more are long forgotten, while Eric is the one who is still remembered. The answer seems to be that his refusal to run on a Sunday has captured the imagination of millions, by being willing to sacrifice his best chance of a gold medal in the 100m – the race he was favourite to win – on the principle that his Christian faith mattered more. Precisely this point was made by Dunky White, a great Scottish runner and coach, at a memorial service for Eric: 'Now to win an Olympic event is a great honour, perhaps the greatest athletic honour. But Eric Liddell is not remembered for this achievement, but as a man who wouldn't run on a Sunday.'

The Olympics began for Eric on 8 July 1924 at Stade Columbes, for many years the home of French rugby. Eric won heat three in the first round of the 200m in 22.2. Later in the day he came second in heat two of the second round, to progress to the semi-finals.

The following day Eric was in the second semi-final. The American Charles Paddock won in 21.8 with Eric second in 21.9, and the final was later that day. Jackson Scholz of the USA won in 21.6, equalling the Olympic record, with Paddock second. Eric was at one stage down in fifth position, but a characteristic late run saw him take the bronze in 21.9. Harold

Abrahams of Great Britain, winner of the 100m, finished last of the six finalists.

The following day Eric was back on the track in the heats of the 400m. He began by winning heat 14 in the first round, in a time of 50.2, and was second to Adrian Paulen (49.0) in the fourth heat of the second round in a time of 49.3. That time was put in perspective by Joseph Imbach of Switzerland, who broke the Olympic record in winning his second-round heat in 48.0. While Liddell was safely through to the semi-final, there was nothing to suggest that he was a potential medallist.

Joseph Imbach's Olympic record did not last long as Horatio Fitch won the first semi-final the next day in a time of 47.8. Guy Butler of Britain, in second place, equalled the previous Olympic record. Eric won the second semi-final in 48.2, with Joseph Imbach in second place.

At about 6.30 p.m. on 11 July 1924, the runners for the 400m final took their places. The track at Stade Columbes was 500m long, meaning that the runners did not complete the normal full lap, but only one bend.

There is an interesting story about Eric and the day of the final. While the incident did actually occur, it has been told in several different and inaccurate forms, and a version of it appears in the film *Chariots of Fire*, with much poetic licence. Even D. P. Thompson, Eric's friend and first biographer, got it wrong in his 1945 account of Eric Liddell's life: 'There is one very revealing incident of the great race at Paris which we owe to Liddell himself,' Thompson wrote. 'I have heard him tell it often. Just before the final, a man came up and slipped something into his hand. It was a piece of paper, and on it were written the words of Scripture: "Them that honour me, I will honour" (1 Samuel 2:30). From what Eric has told me, I believe we owe a debt to that unnamed well-wisher greater than can ever be repaid.' (In *Chariots of Fire*, the giving of the note is attributed to the American athlete Jackson Scholz, who won the 200 m gold medal. When the film came out in 1981, Scholz, then 84, was inundated with mail from people seeking spiritual inspiration which he felt completely ill-equipped to offer.)

In his later book, Thompson gives the correct version:

> Of the many versions of that incident which have been given in print across the years, none is quite accurate. It is to the man actually involved that I am indebted for the true story of what happened.
>
> 'Today', wrote my correspondent on 8 October 1945, 'I saw and purchased a book entitled *Eric Liddell*. I was deeply interested, as being one of the runners' masseurs who attended to Eric and others at Columbes, Paris in 1924 (July). I liked Eric so much, and on the morning of his final 400 metres, I handed him the note mentioned on page 24 of the book. I'm afraid I did not quote the text as written; this is what I put – "In the old book it says, 'He that honours me, I will honour'. Wishing you the best of success always." And I signed it.
>
> 'I gave it to him at the Hotel Modern, Rue de la Republique, Paris and he said, "I'll read it when I get to the Stadium." I saw him start his race and shake hands with his opponents. We said, "He said goodbye to them," for he certainly ran away from them easily. In the dressing room he thanked me for the note, as I and his own trainer, McKerchar, massaged him.'

Eric was drawn in the outside lane – and the race would be run in lanes throughout. The disadvantage of the outside lane is, of course, that the runner has to set his own pace and cannot see any of the other runners until the final stretch of the race.

Liddell set out at a furious pace, unofficially timed at 200 metres in 22.2 – only 0.3 slower than his bronze medal time in the 200m final. He could not quite live up to his claimed strategy for the 400m – running the first half as fast as he could and the second 400m even faster! However, he held off the field to win in 47.6 from Horatio Fitch (48.4) and Guy Butler (48.6).

It was the third Olympic 400m record of the week, and it was also initially recognised as a world record. However, Ted Meredith's previous, faster, run of 47.4 for the 440 yards (3 yards longer than 400m) was later recognised.

On the Sunday following the race, Liddell spoke at the Scottish church in Paris. In a way it was a symbolic gesture, serving as a reminder that our champion's main interest did not lie on the athletic field.

His decision to go to China as a missionary meant that 1925 was his last season in competitive athletics. During this season, he often ran in a town on the Saturday and preached on the Sunday. For example, at one point in 1925 he ran on three consecutive Saturdays in local meets to benefit the host athletic club. On the Sundays following each meet, he preached in a nearby church, always taking time after the services to talk with the young people and sign autographs.

While in China, he did no formal training, but continued to run when the opportunity offered itself. This raises the issue of whether or not he should have been in the British team for 1928. There seems little doubt that he could have made the team.

In the Far Eastern Games at Port Arthur in October 1928, Eric won the 200m in 21.8, and the 400m in 47.8. His achievement is put in context when one notes both times equalled the winning times in the 1928 Amsterdam Olympics of Ray Barbuti in the 400m and Percy Williams in the 200m. Had he been in the 1928 Olympics, Eric would have been a force to contend with. In 1929, Eric had two races against Otto Pelzer (holder of the world records of 500m, 800m and 1500m). Eric beat him in the 400m, but lost the 800m. He also won the North China championship in 1930, but did not compete again after 1930.

The most likely explanation for Eric not being selected for the 1928 Olympics is because no one in the UK knew he was still running. After all, he had stated publicly in 1925 that he was retiring from athletics. Today, Eric's results and times would be recorded in *Athletics Weekly*, and a quick phone call from the British Athletics authorities would clarify his intentions. However, in the 1920s, none of this was possible.

As Eric felt that China was his life's calling, it would probably never have occurred to him to approach the British Olympic officials himself. At this distance in time, it is impossible to be sure what happened. However, it is a reasonable assumption to make that with Eric announcing his retirement from athletics in order to become a missionary in China, the AAAs had no reason to think he was available for selection. They would most likely have thought he was no longer interested in serious athletics, and were probably unaware of his performances in China.

Moreover, if D. P. Thompson was still influential in Eric's life, he would almost certainly have advised him against it. When on his first furlough (1931–2), Eric was keen on doing some running, and Thompson records advising him that 'from every point of view, this would not be wise. He had another race to run after that, and there was to be no doubt at all about the finish.'

Ironically, when Eric was asked if he would be available for the 1932 Olympics, he declined, saying that at 30 he would be too old. Asked in an interview in the early 1930s if he ever regretted giving up running, he replied, 'Oh well, of course it's natural for a chap to think over all that sometimes. But I'm glad I'm at the work I'm engaged in now. A fellow's life is far more for this than the other. Not a corruptible crown but an incorruptible one, you know.'

However, we should certainly not conclude that Eric lost interest in running or thought it unimportant. There is no doubt that he enjoyed running and that he ran to win. Bob Knight recalled hearing him being asked how he often managed to find a little extra, to win races that he seemed to be losing: 'The guest and the assembled company waited for Eric to tell them how he put up a prayer or called on the Lord – something suitably pious, anyway. But he smiled that quiet smile of his – I can picture him now – and he said, "The fact is, I don't like to be beaten." ' Another example of this came when fellow missionary Kenneth McAll invited Eric to go for a jog with him. Eric declined politely, saying, 'When I run, I run to win. I will never jog – but I will go for a stroll.'

Eric certainly saw running as part of his Christian life. He was once asked if he ever prayed that he would win a race. He replied, 'No, I have never prayed that I would win the race. I have, of course, prayed about the athletics meetings, asking that in this, too, God might be glorified.' Sportsmanship was an important part of Eric's attitude to running and he always sought to make every race a fair contest.

Professor Neil Campbell recalled an occasion when he was running a 440-yard race against Eric. Campbell was drawn in the outside lane, and in those days there was no stagger to the lanes in domestic meetings – everyone had to make a mad scramble for the inside of the track after the gun. Eric Liddell, knowing that he was the more experienced of the two, offered to swap lanes, to give his fellow competitor the advantage of the inside track.

Before races he would routinely offer his trowel, which he used to dig footholds, to other sprinters in the race. Once, in a steeplechase race that Eric was watching, one runner knocked over a hurdle. The runner behind could have run through the gap left by the fallen hurdle, but instead he swerved inside in order to jump the hurdle next to the fallen one. Liddell commented, 'That was the finest thing done that day. He did not win – I have forgotten who did – but I can never forget the action. He could not act otherwise; he was led by the spirit of sportsmanship. It was ingrained in him, part of himself. Sport is wonderful! The most wonderful part of it is not the almost superhuman achievements, but the spirit in which it is done. Take away the spirit and it is dead.'

Running was fun for Eric, and he certainly cared if he won or lost, but most important for him was the attitude with which you ran. He was very much influenced by the motto written on the entrance to the University of Pennsylvania: 'In the dust of defeat, as well as in the laurels of victory, there is a glory to be found if one has done his best.'

In China, he served initially as a teacher at the Anglo-Chinese College in Tientsin, the city of his birth, from 1925 to 1937 – except for a period of leave in the UK in 1932. From 1937 onwards he engaged in more specifically evangelistic ministry in Siaochang, a village in the North China plains, and there are many stories of his courage, and willingness to risk his own life to help others in need, during the Japanese occupation of China.

In 1942 Eric, and all foreign missionaries, were sent to Weihsien internment camp – Eric's wife and family had previously been evacuated to safety in Canada. By 1945 Eric was complaining of severe headaches, and he died of a brain tumour on 21 February 1945.

There is one story in particular about Eric in the internment camp that says so much about him. While there, he was responsible for sport and his policy was no Sunday games. When a group of teenagers wanted to play hockey one Sunday, Eric said that they could have the equipment, but he would not be there to umpire. So they decided to organise a hockey game by themselves, despite him – boys against girls. It ended in a free fight because there was no umpire, and on the following Sunday Eric turned out on that field to act as umpire. This incident speaks volumes about Eric. He would not run on a Sunday for an Olympic gold medal, and all the glory in the world, but he was willing to break his unbreakable principle to serve a handful of imprisoned youngsters.

Eric Liddell was a great runner, an Olympic champion, but he gave it all up while still in his prime to serve God in China. He was a man of high principle who is, ironically, remembered more today for the fact that he did not run on a Sunday than for the fact that he won a gold medal.

Olympic record

1924
400m – gold
200m – bronze

4

Kriss Akabusi,
Hurdler Extraordinaire

Kriss Akabusi was the boy who grew up in the children's home;
the boy whose games master said that he had 'no athletic
potential'. However, he was also the man who won three
Olympic medals.

It was in the army that Kriss discovered that he could run,
and it was in 1976 on a training run that he impressed one
of his colleagues who was a serious army runner. This led to
his being entered for a race – which he won – and to his
entering, and winning, the 400m in the Army Junior (under-
18) Championships.

In 1979 he was stationed in Germany and joined a running club. The coach took him aside and told him he had
the potential to go far in athletics, but he needed to take
it more seriously and to give up other sports – Kriss was
often turning up for athletics training hampered by a football
injury!

Back in England, Kriss joined Mike Smith's Southampton
squad, and made rapid progress, being selected by Great Britain
in 1983 for the 4×400m in the World Championships in

Helsinki. Britain won bronze, with Kriss running in the heat and the semi-final, but not selected for the final.

As the 1984 season began, Kriss knew that the Olympics were well within his grasp, if he could but regain his form of the previous season. He started in great form, equalling his personal best in winning the UK Championships in Cwmbran. The following week he broke 46 seconds for the first time (45.85), but could only finish third behind Todd Bennett and Phil Brown. But it was enough to confirm his Olympic selection, conveyed to him in a personally signed letter from the Duke of Edinburgh. Kriss was on his way to the Olympics in Los Angeles!

The experience of the 1984 Olympics was magic for Kriss, and just to be there was the fulfilment of a dream. He recalls, 'I had never been to America before, but I had read all the boys' comics and I was very excited about going to see Spiderman. My first impression was how friendly the Americans were: "Hey man, how are you doing? That's neat!" and so on. It really was a dream come true.'

Kriss ran in the 400m flat. He was there as the third-string British runner, behind Todd Bennett and Phil Brown. However, in the first and second heats he did personal bests, including 45.43, the second fastest ever by a Briton. He was the only Briton to progress to the semi-finals.

He came seventh in the semi-final, in 45.69. How far Kriss was off the pace is shown by Alonzo Babers's gold-medal winning time of 44.27, a full 1.16 seconds faster than his own personal best. Looking back on the event, Kriss now feels that his inexperience was a major factor in his semi-final performance, in that he was over the moon about his personal best in the previous round, and his achievement. He was in a 'go out and enjoy it' frame of mind. The more professional Akabusi of later in his career would have been totally focused on getting in the top four to make the final.

He recognises too that he was a bit 'gob-smacked' by the whole Olympic experience and that his attitude to the 1988 and 1992 Games was much more professional, much more focused than in 1984:

> When you go to the Olympics every four years, you see people you have not seen for a long time. You meet people from all over the world, and the one thing you have in common is that you are all good sportsmen, for the Olympic Games are the meet of champions. There is a friendship, there is a camaraderie, but in the last analysis it is all about competition. You are all friendly and dining together but when your event is approaching you become channelled, very focused on the event ahead. In a way there is a distinction between the first-time Olympian, who is soaking up the atmosphere, and the experienced guys who want to do everything right to try to make the medal rostrum. They have been preparing all year – and longer – just for one moment.

The 4×400m relay in Los Angeles brought Kriss an unexpected silver medal. While none of the rest of the team had even matched Kriss's achievement of reaching the semi-final of the individual 400m, let alone the final, they worked as a team. Kriss (running the first leg), Garry Cook, Todd Bennett and Phil Brown came second in a new British record time of 2:59.13.

Prior to this race, only two relay teams had ever run under three minutes. On this occasion the Australians ran 2:59.7, only to get fourth place. In what the 1985 *International Running Guide* referred to as a 'cracking final', Britain were in fourth place with half a lap to go when Phil Brown overtook first the Australians, and then the Nigerians, to grab the silver-medal position. The performance was a good example of what Kriss calls 'the whole being greater than the sum of the parts', meaning that there are times when a team working together can exceed what would be the sum total of their individual achievements.

It was Kriss's first experience – of many – of getting a medal at a major championship. To stand on the rostrum and receive an Olympic medal and to be acclaimed for your achievement is, indeed, a magic moment:

> For a sportsman to stand on the rostrum, and be recognised by everyone for his achievement, is a very important occasion. The privilege of being in the number one position and seeing the flag of your country go up, and hearing the national anthem – perhaps catching a glimpse of yourself on the big screen, perhaps a re-run of your race. You get a lump in your throat and think 'My word!' People elevate you, but I know who I am and therefore for me to see myself on the big screen, see the flag, hear the national anthem and realise that over 90,000 people in the stadium are sharing that moment, it is a real humbling experience.

The 1984 Olympics were an important step on the ladder for Kriss. He had gone to Los Angeles as an athlete; while there, he had become an Olympian. What is more, he had come back with a silver medal, more than the majority of athletes ever achieve.

It was a very satisfying Olympic debut for Kriss. Two personal bests had been achieved in his individual event, and his contribution to the relay team had helped ensure a silver medal. He comments:

> Pierre de Coubertin, the founder of the modern Olympic Games, said, 'The important thing in the Olympic Games is not to win but to take part; the important thing in life is not the triumph but the struggle; the essential thing is not having conquered but to have fought well.'
>
> However, I was soon to learn the folly of these words in the modern era. I won a silver medal in the British relay quartet, and made the semi-final as an individual. I

certainly had not expected the silver and had only hoped that I would make the semis. I was ecstatic with jubilation.

In 1986, as Kriss approached his twenty-eighth birthday, he reflected on where he was athletically. After the early years of progress, he had hit a plateau, as he had not been able to improve on the personal best he set in the Los Angeles Olympics in the two years since that event. He should have been at his peak now. In reality, he was at a crossroads, unsure of whether he had a future in international athletics.

At 28 he certainly wasn't past his sell-by date, yet if he could no longer be sure of a place in the team for major championships, even for the relay, the question about his future had to be asked. In his own inimitable way he told himself, 'You're a cart-horse, Kriss. You're just a 45.5 man and in the future that's not going to be good enough even to make the relay team.'

Faced with the same evidence, others would have drawn different conclusions. Some would have deluded themselves into thinking that they were better than they really were, that their prospects were OK and they would improve. Others would have been content with what had been achieved so far – the international bests, the Olympic silver medal in the relay, etc. Kriss, in contrast, made a decision and had the determination to follow it through. He faced the issue with total honesty and ruthless logic. His analysis went like this:

- Fact number one: he had been unable to improve his time for the past two seasons. Perhaps he had reached the height of his achievement.
- Fact number two: alongside the established 400m runners like Todd Bennett, Ainsley Bennett and Phil Brown, younger men of great potential were appearing on the scene, for example Derek Redmond and Roger Black.
- Fact number three: in the 400m hurdles, Britain had no outstanding competitor. (In the recent European

Championships the best two Britons, Phil Beattie and Max Robertson, had each come seventh in the semi-final, neither breaking 50 seconds.) David Hemery's British record had stood for 18 years.

Kriss put these three facts into the melting pot, gave it a good stir, and decided that his future lay over the hurdles:

I made the decision to switch to the hurdles. I came to the conclusion that if I continued as a 400 metres [flat] runner, Stuttgart would be my last major championship. Never again would I run in front of a huge crowd and enjoy that special atmosphere. My rivals were young. I could see the next squad coming along and I was out of it. But watching the British guys in the hurdles in the European Championships, there was nobody special. I believed I could make the British team as a hurdler.

Roger Black, Kriss's great friend, commented, 'It's his greatest quality – he's a total realist.'

Kriss approached Mike Whittingham, a former international hurdler who was now coaching. Whittingham instantly recognised Kriss's potential: 'Kriss asked me, "What do you think my potential is?" Now it isn't every day that you are approached by a 400 metre runner who has already run 45.5, who is incredibly dedicated to hard work and to learning a new skill. In view of this I said, "You have the potential to break the British record."' Whittingham recognised that underneath the sunny character and the happy-go-lucky exterior, there was a competitive spirit second to none. Together they set a target of winning the European title in 1990.

During an early race, Kriss was showing well until he hit the ninth hurdle and fell flat on his face on the track. He recalls the incident well: 'In that moment I could have got up and said, "No thanks, this isn't for me," but instead I got up and was more determined than ever that I would work harder until I was successful.' Mike Whittingham warned Kriss that it would take a great deal of hard work, but that didn't frighten Kriss. As Whittingham says, 'Kriss has lifted himself by sheer effort from being a good club athlete to being an international runner.'

So swift had been his progress in the hurdles that one year after switching events he was already in the World Championships – *and* was on form for the event. In the first heat he ran 49.36, only two-hundredths of a second outside his personal best. He also came second in the heat. In the semi-final he came third, but required another personal best, 48.64, to do it. In the final he came seventh in 48.74 which, until the previous day, would have been a personal best. Ed Moses won the race from Danny Harris, beating Kriss by about 10 metres.

There was one supreme irony in the 1988 season. Remember that Kriss had changed events in 1986 because he did not feel confident he would ever again be selected for a major championship in the 400m flat. For the 1988 Olympics, the selectors announced that the AAAs championship would be a kind of Olympic trial, and that anyone who finished first in an event, and who had achieved the Olympic qualifying standard, would gain automatic selection to the Games. Other places would be at the discretion of the selectors.

As UK number one in the hurdles, Kriss was entirely confident of selection for the Olympics. He felt that, with due respect to his fellow competitors, he was unlikely to be pushed in the 400m hurdles. He felt that a fast race on the flat could be more beneficial to his preparations for Seoul, so he entered the 400m flat with this in mind. To his surprise, he won the race in a personal best time of 44.93. His previous best of 45.43, set in the 1984 Olympics, had stood for four years.

His own reaction was: 'That gave me immense pleasure! All of a sudden here I was, now a 400m hurdler, but still with a lot of passion for the flat, finally achieving my great ambition of breaking 45 seconds! I'm satisfied. I don't need to run another 400, and probably won't.' Kriss was quick to announce that the race had been a training exercise and that he wanted to run the hurdles in Seoul, and not take up his automatic 400m flat place in the team.

In the four years since the Los Angeles Olympics, a great deal had happened in Kriss's life. As well as switching to hurdles, he had also become a Christian, and 1988 was a lot more serious for him than the previous Olympics. In 1984 he had gone to enjoy himself and to do the best he could. By 1988 he had sufficient credibility in athletics to expect to make the final, and possibly achieve one of the first three places.

In the event, despite a slight injury problem, he made the final, but only just – coming fourth in his semi-final, with four reaching the final. In a television interview he said of his injury, 'I'll be OK so long as all the Christians out there keep praying.' In the final he came sixth in a time of 48.69, which was probably all that he could have expected at that stage of his development as a hurdler. His time was almost identical to the one he had run in Rome in the World Championship the previous year – 48.69 to 48.74, and only five-hundredths of a second off his personal best.

He had the satisfaction, too, of being the first European to finish. The race was won by Andre Phillips, with the legendary Ed Moses third – only Moses' second defeat in eleven years. Afterwards, Andre Phillips said, 'I watched Edwin Moses in the 1976 Olympics in Montreal and I've been chasing him ever since.' Incidentally, Kriss was once asked if he had ever run with Ed Moses. Quick as a flash he replied: 'No, I can't say I have. I've been in the same races as him. I've run behind him, but I can't say that I've run with him!'

The 1988 Olympic 4×400m relay saw a reasonable performance, but no medal for Britain. Kriss ran the second leg in the team, which finished fifth in exactly 3.2 seconds, nearly three seconds slower than in 1984. *Athletics Today* reported: 'Any chance of a medal was lost when anchorman Phil Brown was obstructed as he set off. The loss of Derek Redmond through injury proved too great a blow, even though Brian Whittle,

Kriss Akabusi, Todd Bennett and Phil Brown ran their hearts out.'

There had been a meeting of Christian athletes on the night before the 4×400m relay final, with three of the finalists represented – Kriss Akabusi from the UK, Innocent Egbunike of Nigeria, and America's Danny Everett. As each one prayed, Egbunike's prayer was, 'Lord, I don't ask that I should win tomorrow, but please, please don't let me finish behind Akabusi.' The meeting ended in chaotic laughter. (For the record, Nigeria were seventh to Britain's fifth.)

Kriss's own end-of-term report on the 1988 season was, 'I confirmed myself by being the first European to finish at the Olympic Games, running 48.69 seconds in sixth position.'

In 1990, Kriss won the 400m hurdles in the Commonwealth Games and European Championships, setting a new British record of 47.92 to beat David Hemery's time, which had stood since 1968. In the 1991 World Championships, Kriss took bronze, setting a new British record in 47.91. At the 1991 World Championships, he also ran the last leg in Britain's epic victory over the USA in the 4×400m relay in a European and Commonwealth record of 2:57.53.

By the time the 1992 Olympics in Barcelona came along, Kriss was 33 – and it would clearly be his last Olympics. What he wrote in the *Guardian* diary summed up the significance of the event: 'On your marks . . . four years of blood, sweat and tears all hang on the performance of this day. There is no room for error. No second chance.' Barcelona was, of course, Akabusi's third Olympics, after Los Angeles in 1984 and Seoul in 1988. He already had an Olympic silver medal, and his medal collection included Commonwealth, European and World Championships gold medals. Only the Olympic gold was needed to complete the set.

In the years from 1988 to 1992 Kriss's stock had risen. As well as the medals he had collected (which also included a bronze in the World Championships), he was also ranked third in the world. However, Kriss was now 33 – nearer 34 if the truth be known – could he continue to improve or would age finally catch up with him? Certainly this was his last chance at that elusive Olympic gold medal, and the focus of the last four years was on this moment.

Everything he had done in 1992 was in preparation for 6 August 1992. The training, the self-discipline, the self-denial – all to be in prime condition for the first week in August. The programme of races had been carefully chosen to bring him to peak fitness at just the right time: not too early, nor too late. If Kriss Akabusi were to gain an Olympic gold medal, it was now or never. Those thoughts crowded in as he went to his marks and sought to focus all his energy and attention on the race ahead.

Kriss's final preparations were in Monte Carlo, where training went well. He arrived in Barcelona on 29 July, ready to do the business, ready to rock and roll.

The Olympic 400m hurdles event consists of three races in five days – heat, semi-final and final. The task is to make the final – not to fall at the first hurdle, so to speak.

Forty-seven competitors ran in seven heats on 3 August. Kriss won his heat in 48.98 and two days later he won his semi-final in a much quicker time of 48.01. Winthrop Graham won the other semi-final in 47.62, with Kevin Young second, also under 48 seconds.

Kriss's assessment of his work so far was:

When I went to the Olympic Games in 1992 I was expecting to get a medal. I had now had a lot of experience and had become the best hurdler in Europe. So I went to the Barcelona with a real chance of picking up the Big G – the gold medal. In 1984 it had been enough to be there. In 1988 I was satisfied to make the final, but in 1992 I felt that I had a real chance of winning gold. As the Games started I got quite excited as I thought maybe I could win this time round. In the heats and the semi-final nobody looked that terrific.

So Kriss had avoided the pitfalls of injury and loss of form, and had successfully made his way through to the final. He went to bed on 5 August knowing that all the preparation had been great, but now was the time to do the business.

The athletes get to the stadium a couple of hours before the race, and go through their warm-up routines in the practice area. Then it is a case of waiting to be called to the track. The athletes set up their starting blocks, try them out, make any last-minute adjustments. It is time to get down to business.

Kriss continued: 'On the day of the final, I was pretty excited – this was it – the finals had come! I got back to my marks and I was very confident actually. In the heats I had run particularly well and I felt very good and thought maybe I could win this time.' He added mischievously, 'I don't believe in the divine right of kings' – a clear reference to his own hopes of a win.

'The starter says, "Competitors on your marks." Your heart is pounding and you look around. For me, I always say a little prayer: "Well, Lord, here I am. I have prepared myself the best I can. Let's just do it." I'm thinking, "There's no ducking out now, so let's just do it." That's the way I control and prepare myself.'

On your marks! Get set! Bang! The 1992 Olympic final of the 400m hurdles is under way! Kriss takes up the story:

I went as hard as I could, but by the time I got to hurdle 5 the American, Kevin Young, came flying past me and I thought, 'Oh my gosh, I'm having a bad one.' At this point it would have been easy to panic – either to try to catch Young and burn myself out or to give up. Then as I got round the bend I worked really hard and I realised I wasn't running that bad because it was only Kevin Young who was ahead of me.

I got to the last hurdle late and Winthrop Graham came past me as well, but by the last 100 metres I knew that if

I didn't make any mistakes, I was going to hold on to my bronze medal. I think by the time I got to hurdle 10 that's all I was thinking about – holding on to my bronze medal – rather than wanting to catch anybody else.

I had been very confident in the final, but it did not go according to plan for one man ran a fantastic race. Even though I broke the British record yet again, Kevin Young broke the world record. Then I realised that, for me, the game was over. I did not expect to lose to a world record. I never expected Edwin Moses' record to be broken in my generation. I couldn't believe it! But in the end, as history records, I came third, and now I'm very happy that I came third and got a medal.

That race was undoubtedly one of the highlights of the 1992 Olympics. While the race belonged to Kevin Young, who smashed the world record of the great Ed Moses on his way to the gold medal, Kriss still ran faster than ever before in his life. To crown a great career with an Olympic medal and another British record was a tremendous achievement. As Kriss often puts it when talking about the race, 'That day proved that I could not be the best. I had to be satisfied with just doing my best.' He adds, 'Kevin Young and I had one thing in common that day. His gold medal and my bronze each represented the best that we could be in our field of expertise.'

Despite his disappointments, Kriss had let no one down. To return home from the Olympic Games with one bronze medal, let alone two, made him the envy of the vast majority of the competitors. He could approach his retirement with contentment.

After the 400m hurdles came the relay. Kriss continues:

After our gold medal in the World Championships at Tokyo in 1991, a great deal was expected of us at the Olympics. But by the time we came to the relay, we had a few tired legs out there and I think, to be honest, we knew that it was not going to be as easy as last time. It was difficult to win in Tokyo, but we knew we had the ability to win because the Americans did not have their best team in Tokyo. They were very complacent, they thought they could put any four out to beat us.

This time round the Americans had four guys who could go under 44 seconds, and we didn't have one guy who could do that. We'd lost Derek Redmond, who was the British record holder, a week earlier. So we knew we were up against it. We were very tired when we got there. I did not think I would be the best man to run this time and tried to get out of it – there were a couple of other young guys who hadn't run during that week. But in the end, we came third. We felt we should have got silver, but that was the measure of how tired we really were.

Still, for the boy with 'no athletic potential', three Olympics, five finals and three medals was not a bad result.

Olympic record

1984 Los Angeles
4 Aug: 400m heat – 1st, 45.64 (pb)
5 Aug: 400m quarter-final – 3rd, 45.43 (pb)
6 Aug: 400m semi-final – 7th, 45.69 (pb)
11 Aug: 4×400m final – 2nd, 2:59.13 (European record)

1988 Seoul
23 Sep: 400m hurdles heat – 2nd, 49.62
24 Sep: 400m hurdles semi-final – 4th, 49.22
25 Sep: 400m hurdles final – 6th, 48.69
1 Oct: 4×400m final – 5th, 3:02.00

1992 Barcelona
3 Aug: 400m hurdles heat – 1st, 48.98
5 Aug: 400m hurdles semi-final – 1st, 48.01
6 Aug: 400m hurdles final – 3rd, 47.82 (British record)
8 Aug: 4×400m final – 3rd, 2:59.73

This chapter was written on the basis of numerous conversations with Kriss – often on a golf course. Some of this chapter was previously published in my book Kriss *(HarperCollins, 1996).*

5

Great Olympians: Six of the Best

The Olympic Games have been on the scene for nearly 3000 years, and in that time there have been so many epic performances, so many great Olympic champions. There are world records by the dozen, tales of courage and determination aplenty. Therefore it is an invidious task to choose just six. I am certain that my six are worthy of inclusion, but so are many champions that I have had to leave out. Making such a selection is essentially a subjective decision.

I have gone for a mixture of sports and periods, but before considering each one in detail, let me justify my choice. They are all different in their achievement, but similar in the *level* of their achievement:

- **Lasse Viren** – it is beyond almost all of us to win one Olympic gold medal in a long-distance athletics event, but Lasse Viren won two. Four years later, he successfully defended both titles.
- **Jesse Owens** was a story of triumph over adversity and conducting oneself with dignity in the face of Hitler's blatant racism.

- **Daley Thompson** – to master 10 disciplines, and be the best in the world at it, made Daley Thompson simply the most complete athlete of his time.
- **Mark Spitz** won seven gold medals in one Olympics – need I say more!
- **Steve Redgrave** – if Mark Spitz won seven gold medals in a week, it took Steve Redgrave 16 years to win his five. Redgrave took a rowing gold at five successive Olympics.
- **Carl Lewis** was the winner of nine track and field gold medals.

Lasse Viren

Lasse Viren of Finland came to fame in 1972 when, halfway through the final of the 10,000m, he and another runner tripped. However, Lasse was quickly back on his feet and soon closed the gap on the leading group of runners. He ran the final lap in 56.4 seconds to win the gold medal, and even broke the world record! To set a new world record is a great achievement; to set a world record in a race in which you have fallen is amazing.

Viren's preparation had been meticulous. Before the race, he and his coach had gone through the list of runners, identifying the potential winners and discussing the tactics they were likely to use and how to counter them. For example, Viren knew that David Bedford liked to start off his races at breakneck speed. So in preparation for the Olympics, Viren had run a 5000m race, starting with a 59-second lap, in order to see how this affected him.

One of Viren's great strengths was the ability to impose himself on a race. He was not the fastest sprinter in the world, but seemed to be able to judge the pace of a race in order to take the sting out of the fast finishers.

He described the tension of his first Olympic final: 'It was a new situation for me. I did not know what would happen in that giant Olympic stadium.' When he won, it lifted the pressure:

'After my first gold it was much easier. I had already one gold in my pocket, so I had nothing to lose and was able to relax.' He added that he was so busy celebrating that he did not have time to get nervous about the 5000m and he won that as well.

In Montreal in 1976, he retained his 10,000m and 5000m titles. The 10,000m was reasonably straightforward, but the 5000m was more of a battle. With 1000m to go, he hit the front and was strong enough to keep going and to win. Two days after the 5000m final he decided to run his first-ever marathon. Amazingly – considering that in only the previous week he had run Olympic heats and finals in both the 5000m and 10,000m events – he finished fifth.

He ran in the 1980 Olympics, but only managed a fifth in the 10,000m event. He is remembered as one of the legends of long-distance running, with four Olympic gold medals and three world records.

Olympic record

1972
5000m – gold 13:26.4 (Olympic record)
10,000m – gold 27:38.4 (world and Olympic records)

1976
5000m – gold 13:24.76
10,000m – gold 27:40.38
Marathon – 5th

1980
10,000m – 5th

Jesse Owens

James Cleveland Owens was born in 1913. When a teacher asked him his name on his first day of school, he replied, 'J. C. Owen.' She thought he said 'Jesse', and the name stuck.

When coach Charlie Riley saw him run for the first time, he immediately recognised the raw, yet natural, talent that young Jesse had, and immediately invited him to run for the track team. At Cleveland East Technical High School Jesse became a track star, tying the world record in the 100-yard dash with a time of 9.4.

When he went to Ohio State University, he experienced shocking racism and was required to live off-campus with other African-American athletes. When he travelled with the team, Jesse could either order a take-away or eat at 'blacks only' restaurants. Likewise, he slept in 'blacks only' hotels.

In 1935 Jesse set three world records and tied a fourth, all in a span of about 70 minutes. Ironically, earlier in the week he had fallen down a flight of stairs, injuring his back. Hmm – pity he hadn't been fit that day or he could really have shown them what he could do! In this kind of form it was inevitable that he would get into the US team for the 1936 Olympics in Berlin.

Jesse was triumphant in the 100-metres dash, the 200-metres dash and the long jump; he was also a key member of the 400-metres relay team that won the gold medal. In all but one of these events, Jesse set Olympic records. He was the first American in the history of Olympic track and field to win four gold medals in a single Olympics.

Adolf Hitler's plans to use the Games to demonstrate the superiority of the Master Race came a cropper, for by the end the German crowds were cheering Jesse to victory.

Not that Jesse was involved in anything but a sports event, and he said afterwards, 'I wanted no part of politics. And I wasn't in Berlin to compete against any one athlete. The purpose of the Olympics, anyway, was to do your best. As I'd learned long ago from Charles Riley, the only victory that counts is the one over yourself.' He did have one slightly cynical view of his success, however: 'After I came home from the 1936 Olympics with my four medals, it became increasingly apparent that everyone was going to slap me on the back, want to shake my hand or have me up to their suite. But no one was going to offer me a job.'

The cancellation of the 1940 and 1944 Olympics as a result of the war deprived Jesse of the opportunity to defend his titles. Nearly 70 years on, he is remembered as one of the greatest Olympians of all time.

Olympic record

1936

100m – gold, 10.3 seconds (tying the world record)

Long jump – gold, 26 ft 5¼ in (Olympic record)

200m – 20.7 seconds (Olympic record)

4×100m relay (first leg) in 39.8 seconds (Olympic and world records)

Daley Thompson

In the ancient Olympics, the pentathletes were much admired for their combination of strength and speed, and Daley Thompson follows in that tradition. He is arguably the best decathlete of the modern age, and his record speaks for itself:

- Olympic Champion in 1980 and 1984
- World Champion in 1983
- European Champion in 1982 and 1986
- Commonwealth Champion in 1978, 1982 and 1986
- He broke the world record four times
- He was unbeaten in 12 consecutive decathlons, 1978–87

As well as the multi-event achievements, he twice won medals in 4×100m relays (Commonwealth Games and European Championships) and came sixth in the Commonwealth Games pole-vault.

At the 1982 Commonwealth Games, he declined the honour of carrying his country's flag at the opening ceremony in order to preserve his strength. He explained, 'Competition is my life – winning is my only goal. Everything I do is directed toward that end and I will never permit anything to jeopardise it . . . Since winning is the only prize anybody cares about in this world, I would like people to know what it costs.'

In 1984 he won his second Olympic title by 25 points after an epic battle with Jürgen Hingsen of West Germany. It was a close battle over the first seven events, but then Thompson pulled away with strong performances in the pole-vault and the javelin. With the gold medal secure, Thompson needed to run the final event, the 1500m, in a time of 4:34.98 to break Hingsen's world record. Thompson exasperated the crowd by easing up at the finish line and stopping the clock at 4:35.00. Two years later, IAAF officials re-examined the photo timer results and discovered that Thompson had completed the 110m hurdles in 14.33 seconds rather than 14.34 seconds. They then added one more point to his Olympic total and he was given a belated share of the world record.

Olympic record

1976 – 18th
1980 – gold
1984 – gold
1988 – 4th

Mark Spitz

Mark Spitz won seven swimming gold medals in the 1972 Munich Olympics, but the real story begins in 1968. In the two years leading up to 1968, Spitz had broken 28 US records and 10 world records and he approached the Olympics full of confidence.

As world record holder he was a clear favourite in the 100m butterfly. However, he went off too fast and, normally a devastating finisher, he found he had nothing left by the end, and fellow countryman Doug Russell overtook him to take gold. In the 200m butterfly, Mark's time was fully eight seconds outside his world record. He won two gold medals, but it was back to the drawing-board.

Then in 1972 the dream came true when he won the 200m butterfly, breaking the world record. The same day he swam the last leg of the 4×100m freestyle relay, leading the US team to gold. Then it was gold in the 200m freestyle – another world record, followed by the 100m butterfly, again a world record. An hour after the 100m butterfly, he helped the USA to gold in the 4×200m freestyle relay.

The 100m freestyle was a magnificent contest, with Spitz just holding off Jerry Heidenreich for a sixth gold – and the inevitable world record. Gold medal number seven came as he saw the USA home in the medley relay. He was the first person to win seven gold medals in a single Olympic Games.

Still only aged 22, Spitz retired from swimming after the Munich Games. However, in 1992, at the age of 41, Spitz tried to make a comeback for the Barcelona Olympics, but failed to beat the qualifying limit. In his career, he broke world records 26 times.

Olympic record

1968
100m freestyle – bronze, 53.0
100m butterfly – silver, 56.4 (world record)
4×100m freestyle relay – gold, 3:31.7 (world record)
4×200m freestyle relay – gold, 7:52.1 (world record)

1972
100m freestyle – gold, 51.22 (world record)
100m butterfly – gold, 54.27 (world record)
200m freestyle – gold 1:52.78 (world record)
200m butterfly – gold 2:00.7 (world record)
4×100m freestyle relay – gold 3:26.42 (world record)

4×200m freestyle relay – gold 7:35.78 (world record)
4×100m medley relay – gold 3:48.16 (world record)

Steve Redgrave

Sir Steve Redgrave is simply the greatest Olympian that Britain has ever produced. After striking gold in Sydney, he became our only competitor ever to have won gold medals at five consecutive Olympic Games.

In addition to his Olympic successes he had four unbeaten seasons from 1993 to 1996, and won his ninth World Championship gold in August 1999, his first having been in 1986. Other honours in the sport include the Henley Royal Regatta Diamond Sculls several times, the Silver Goblets a record seven times, and being a triple Commonwealth gold medallist at Edinburgh in 1986, winning the Single Sculls, Coxless Pairs, and Coxed Fours.

The fifth Olympic gold medal almost did not happen as after the 1996 Olympics he announced his retirement, saying, 'If anyone sees me get in a boat again they have permission to shoot me.' He changed his mind, though, announcing in 1997 that he had decided to carry on competing through to the Millennium Games in Sydney – and the rest is history.

No Olympian in the history of the modern Games had achieved five successive golds in an endurance sport. His achievements are all the more remarkable as he suffers from diabetes. Between 1986 and 1999, during every year in which a World Championship was held, Redgrave won at least one medal, including the nine golds mentioned above.

Olympic record

1984
Gold in the Coxed Fours

1988
Gold with Andy Holmes in the Coxless Pairs
Bronze medal, Coxed Pair

1992
Gold with Matthew Pinsent in the Coxless Pairs

1996
Gold with Matthew Pinsent in the Coxless Pairs

2000
Gold in the Coxless Fours

Carl Lewis

Carl Lewis grew up in New Jersey and was introduced to track and field as a schoolboy. When the 1936 legend Jesse Owens came to an athletics meeting near where the nine-year-old Lewis lived, the latter was inspired. He recalls, 'It was an incredible experience for me. It was amazing. I was able to have a connection with someone who was so revered and such an incredible performer.'

Lewis established himself as the best athlete in the world in 1983 when he won the 100m, 4×100m and the long jump at the World Championships.

At the 1984 Olympic Games, Lewis duplicated Jesse Owens's 1936 feat by winning four gold medals. Never a great starter, he showed an amazing finishing burst in the 100m, being clocked at 28 m.p.h. when he hit the tape and winning by 8 feet, the largest margin in the history of the Olympic event. In 1988 he won the 100m, after Ben Johnson was disqualified (see Chapter 2), and two other gold medals.

By the 1992 Olympics, Lewis's star seemed to be in decline. He failed to qualify for either of the sprints and won a spot on the 4×100m relay team only because another runner was injured. However, he won his seventh and eighth gold medals in the long jump and the relay. For the fifth time in his career, he anchored a team to a world record in the 4×100m relay.

At 35, Lewis returned to the Olympics, competing only in the long jump. He won it for the fourth time, giving him nine gold medals during his career.

His achievements, though, have been cast under something of a shadow by persistent rumours of covered-up failed drugs tests.

Olympic record

1984
100m – gold, 9.99
200m – gold, 19.8 (Olympic record)
Long jump – gold, 8.54 metres
4×100m relay – gold, 37.83 (world record)

1988
100m – gold, 9.92
200m – silver, 19.79
4×100m relay – disqualified
Long jump – gold, 8.72 metres

1992
4×100m relay – gold, 37.40 (world record)
Long jump – gold, 8.67 metres

1996
Long jump – gold, 8.50 metres

6

Steph Cook,
Doctor and Pentathlete

Steph Cook went to the Sydney Olympics as a doctor who had become good at her hobby, wanting to see how far she could go. She went to enjoy the once-in-a-lifetime experience, and never guessed what effect it would have on her life.

Steph was just an average schoolgirl – hard-working and reasonably sporty. Her first love was horse-riding, but she also enjoyed running at school. 'I was never much good at sprinting,' she recalls, 'but whenever we did any kind of long-distance running I would be able to keep going for longer than anyone else, and used to do quite well. But I was certainly no remarkable athlete or anything like that.'

When she left school, Steph studied medicine, first at Cambridge and then Oxford. In Cambridge she met a number of veterinary students who competed in the modern pentathlon, and even though she declined their invitations to join them, a seed had been sown.

During her years in Cambridge another seed was sown and flourished. She grew up in a Christian family and went to church at Christmas and Easter, but that was about it, although

71

she can remember from an early age having her New Testament by her bed and reading bits of it:

> It was as if I knew there was someone there, watching out for me and looking after me. When I was 17, I was walking to a good friend's house with her and she started questioning me about what I believed. It was the first time anyone had challenged me to think about spiritual things.
>
> It started me thinking and questioning what I really did believe and what my own faith was. My friend went to a youth group in Cambridge and I started going with her. There was never one defining moment when I thought, 'Yes, that's it! Everything has changed.' I think my faith has always been there, although it hadn't been clarified in my own mind, but during that period everything started to make more sense.

Between school and university, Steph spent six months in Israel. It was an important time of consolidating her faith, as it placed the biblical accounts of Jesus within their historical context.

Back in Cambridge as an undergraduate, there was plenty of teaching, fellowship and encouragement at her church, the university Christian Union and college chapel services. But these were not the only places where Steph expressed her faith: 'I wanted to be a Christian in other situations, rather than being totally involved in Christian things. I was involved in sport and tried to be a Christian representative, to be a witness as much through my actions as my words.'

When Steph commenced her clinical medical studies in Oxford, running was her main sport; and shortly after arriving at Lincoln College, Oxford, she saw a poster in college inviting people to try modern pentathlon.

Modern pentathlon consists of horse-riding, fencing, shooting, running and swimming – usually all held on one day. The sport was born out of the bravery of a young French cavalry

The astonishing spectacle of the Olympic Games is demonstrated by these images from the opening ceremonies at Atlanta (1996) and Sydney (2000)

©Mark Shearman

©Mark Shearman

Two great Olympic moments in contrast – Ben Johnson's disgrace
and Seb Coe's glory

Eric Liddell's famous win in the 1924 Olympics' 400 metres final

Steph Cook with her modern pentathlon gold medal (Sydney 2000)

Barcelona 1992: Kriss Akabusi on his way to the bronze medal
in the 400 metres hurdles

Michelle Akers in action (Atlanta 1996)

The US soccer team celebrate their victory in Atlanta

South African swimmer Penny Heyns prepares to compete

©Mark Shearman

©Mark Shearman

One of Britain's most successful modern-day Olympians:
Jonathan Edwards in action, and celebrating, at the Sydney games

Amanda Borden leads the US gymnastics team to gold in Atlanta

officer in Napoleon's ranks during the Franco-Prussian war in the nineteenth century, or so the legend goes. The officer was sent, on a horse he had never ridden before, to deliver a message. En route, he faced a fencing duel, shot the soldier who killed his horse, and ran to continue his mission, finally swimming across a river to complete it. Pierre de Coubertin, the French founding father of the modern Olympics, was so moved by the tale that he came up with the idea of a pentathlon, which was introduced at the 1912 Games.

Steph was on her way to international recognition as a runner. She had also done quite a bit of riding, but had not swum competitively since school and had never shot nor fenced. Despite this, she attended a few training sessions and took part in a varsity match for novices – and won. However, at this stage her top priority was her studies; she was running seriously, but no more than dabbling in pentathlon.

In 1997, her final year at university, Steph represented Oxford in four sports – athletics, cross-country, fencing and modern pentathlon. She gained her first England running vest for cross-country, and was also selected to compete for Great Britain in modern pentathlon. But of course there was also the matter of her medical finals to be fitted into the schedule.

She came fourth in her first international pentathlon competition, but it was a rather low-key event. The following week she competed in a World Cup event in Hungary and, when she came fifth, people began to notice her.

When Steph started work as a junior doctor, she was an international pentathlete, but had so far missed out on competing in a major championship, having been a non-travelling reserve for the British team for both the European and World Championships in 1997.

'I was so close and felt I deserved a chance,' she says. 'Having got so close, I wanted to take it one step further. In retrospect, if I had been selected for the World Championships, I might have thought that was enough and not gone any further. As it was, I felt I had not really fulfilled my potential.'

The following year, while working long hours as a junior doctor, she continued training and competing. She was selected for the 1998 World Championships in Mexico, coming eighth individually, as well as gaining team silver and relay bronze medals.

In 1999, Steph Cook was the British modern tetrathlon champion (pentathlon without the riding); and in the modern pentathlon European Championships, she was tenth in the individual competition as well as taking a team silver. At the World Championships she won a team silver and a relay gold.

A chance meeting with a consultant surgeon led to the offer of doing medical research, which was more flexible than a clinical post for her training and competition. A chance meeting it may have been, but for Steph it was also 'God opening a door. There were a few things that happened that led me to try and take pentathlon a bit further. This was a chance meeting, but I believe God's hand was in it. I moved to Guildford, not really knowing what to expect and feeling quite apprehensive. I was wondering what I was doing there, but it seemed to be what God was telling me to do.'

Steph then discovered that she qualified for a Sports Council lottery grant which would enable her to train full-time for the 2000 Olympics. In March 2000, she secured her Olympic qualification by winning gold at the Mexico World Cup. She completed her preparations by taking the individual silver medal (plus relay gold and team silver) at the European Championships in Hungary, and followed these with a ninth place and two team silvers at the World Championships.

She set out for the Olympics determined to make the most of the experience:

My preparation for Sydney had gone well and my competitions had been consistently good. Just after we arrived in Sydney, the new world rankings came out and I found that I was ranked joint number one in the world!

Before that I had sat down and thought, 'What do I

really want to achieve in Sydney? What would be a good thing for me to achieve?' I remember thinking that whatever happened in the Olympics, it would be nice at some stage to be world number one. I had been in the top 10 for some time but to be number one would be something quite special! I wasn't expecting it at this point. It was quite strange and, to start with, it seemed to put increased pressure and expectation upon me.

But I turned it around and started using it in a positive way. It meant that I had performed consistently well during the year and there was no reason why it shouldn't be the same in Sydney.

As she left for Sydney, Steph took with her a book of Bible quotes that a friend had given her, organised into a verse for each day of the training camp and the Games. 'It was lovely for me to have them each day as a focus, and to build them into my quiet times. God was constantly there as a focus for the day. I find it very important to be disciplined in my Christian life and to try to have regular quiet times each day. It can be difficult when you are away and don't have the usual fellowship and encouragement from a church.'

Steph's first memorable moment from the Olympics happened as they began: 'We were very fortunate to have the opportunity to go to the opening ceremony. Many of the Great Britain team were still based on the Gold Coast, and team policy was for athletes not to travel to Sydney just for the opening ceremony. But the pentathlon team thought it would be beneficial for us to go down and get a feel for the atmosphere and experience the village before returning the following week for competition. I'm sure it was the right thing to do. It was an amazing experience to walk into the stadium as part of the British team.'

With the fun over, then came business. There are no heats in the modern pentathlon: the 24 competitors simply compete on the day until one of them is crowned champion. In track events, the 100m final lasts less than 10 seconds – one mistake and you are gone. In contrast, the modern pentathlon Olympic final consists of 20 pistol shots, 23 sword fights, a 200-metre swim, a round of show jumping and a 3000-metre run. One mistake makes little difference – no one can be perfect at everything. Endurance is what is needed. Fortunately, Steph had developed a lot of endurance while working long hours as a doctor.

On Sunday 1 October at 6.45 a.m., the event got under way. Despite the early start, there was quite a crowd in the arena. The first event is the shooting. Steph scored 178 target points; the leader had 185. 'I was pleased with the shooting,' she says. 'It was within the range of what I expected to shoot. I had hoped for 180, so 178 wasn't too bad. That put me in eighth place and still in touch with the leaders.'

After a one-hour break, the fencing began. The change from shooting to fencing is difficult. Mentally the competitors want to be calm and controlled for the shooting, and then aggressive for the fencing. Not being a naturally aggressive person, Steph has to work hard to psyche herself up. This is not her strong event, so holding her own was the target.

Each person fences the other 23 competitors. Steph started with a win over team-mate Kate Allenby, but lost her next four fights: 'When I found myself five hits into the competition and four down, that was the only time in the whole day I felt anxious. It was make-or-break time. I needed a mental turn-around. I needed to go into the sixth bout with the same confidence I had started with.' She finished the fencing with 10 victories, slipping to fourteenth place overall.

'I was pleased with how the fencing had gone,' Steph says. 'It was solid. I had been able to hold my own against the other competitors as far as points were concerned. But because I had dropped to fourteenth place, I knew that anyone who didn't know me, or what I was capable of in the later events, would write me off at that stage. That didn't worry me. I was just pleased that I had my best events to look forward to.'

By midday the competitors were at the Olympic pool. There are three heats of eight swimmers, graded according to past performances. Steph was in the first heat and swam a personal best: 2.26. She says: 'I was hoping for 2.25, but you can't grumble about that.' She still lay in fourteenth place overall, but had narrowed the gap.

'I knew that as long as I had a decent ride I could be in with a chance. In pentathlon it's never worth thinking about where you might end up until the riding is over, because that can shake things up completely.'

For the show jumping, competitors were confronted with 12 Australian horses they had never seen before. Each horse goes around the course with two competitors. The event is harsh. Three competitors were eliminated and got no points at all; their medal hopes were destroyed.

Steph drew a horse called Wagga-Wagga. Her partner rode first and, while Steph watched, collected several penalties. Steph says: 'I was thinking, "Now I have got to get on this horse and try to make it go better than that." I thought I would do OK, but my chances of a medal seemed to be slipping away. I thought the horse would probably knock too many poles down. I spent most of the 20 minutes' preparation time [which each competitor is allowed, to get to know the horse] trying to calm it down. I didn't have many muscles left in my arms after the ride, as the horse was very strong. I was thrilled to come away with only two fences down.' This moved her up to eighth position.

Just before 5 p.m., the final event, the 3000m, began. Points convert to time. The leader starts first, then everyone else so many seconds later, according to the points they have accumulated in the previous four events. So Steph started 49 seconds behind the leader. She says:

> Over the summer, in other competitions, I had made up quite a lot of seconds on other people. I believed that if I was within a minute of the leaders, I stood a chance of running myself into the medals. What you have no control

over, though, is how fast the other people are going to run. For me the crucial person was Emily deRiel, the leader. I knew she had been training at altitude before arriving in Australia, and I had not seen her run since the World Championships in June. All I could do was to run my own race and hope it would be enough. The important thing for me was to pace the race right. If I could do that then, God willing, I would still be able to pass Emily at the end.

By the first corner, Steph had passed the girl in seventh place. After 500 metres she had cut the lead to 33 seconds. By halfway she was fourth; then she passed Mary Beth Iagorashvili. 'That was one of the most exciting moments,' she remembers, 'when I knew I had a medal. It was hurting quite a lot at that stage and it was quite tempting to leave it there and settle for a bronze medal, but then I thought, "No one will forgive me if I don't really go for it." '

With 500 metres to go, Steph passed Kate Allenby to move into second place and, with 300 metres left, overtook Emily deRiel to take the lead, holding it to win by two seconds! At 5.30 p.m., almost 12 hours after the competition started, the British national anthem was played as the gold medal was presented to Steph Cook.

Across the main road from the baseball stadium – where the afternoon events had been taking place – the men's marathon was also finishing, and that was immediately followed by the closing ceremony. There was no way that Steph was going to miss out on that final victory parade!

She had set out for Sydney as a doctor who was rather good at her hobby, but returned home as a celebrity. She was totally unprepared for the demands on her time. There were the television appearances, endless interviews, awards ceremonies, charity functions, not to mention the shock of being recognised in the supermarket or being stopped in the street.

Some of it has been great fun, some of it downright exhausting. 'I cope in the only way I know how – by being me. It was incredibly difficult after Sydney. Overnight it felt as though my life was totally turned upside down, and yet I was still the same person with the same principles and values as always.' Keeping her focus right has helped too. 'When I took up modern pentathlon, it was obvious that God had given me gifts for the sport. I just tried to use the ability God had given me to the full, and hopefully bring some glory to his name in the process.'

Steph continued to compete in 2001, winning the World Championship. Now she has returned to her medical career full time, and the 2000 Olympic Games are just a memory – but *what* a memory!

Olympic record

2000
Gold

This chapter was written on the basis of an exclusive interview with Steph in December 2000. The author also had the amazing experience of being present at the Olympic pentathlon from 6.30 a.m. to after 6.00 p.m. on that amazing day in Sydney. A version of this chapter was included in The Winning Edge *by Peter Furst (Lime Grove House Publishing, Sydney, 2000).*

7

Michelle Akers, Triumph in Adversity

Michelle Anne Akers is simply the most successful football player in the history of the women's game, and her achievements on their own would fill a book. She played in the USA's first-ever women's football international in 1985 and most of the games during the following 15 years, until injury forced her to pull the plug on an illustrious career, just prior to the 2000 Olympics.

The following facts help to express the magnitude of her achievements:

- 153 caps for the USA
- 105 goals
- All-time leading goal-scorer in the World Cup – 12 goals
- Named in 1999 World Cup all-star team
- Received the FIFA Order of Merit in 1998
- Member of FIFA Commission along with Pele, Franz Beckenbauer, Michel Platini and Bobby Charlton
- First American woman player to have a boot contract

And then there is the small matter of the 1996 Olympics – but we will come to that later.

The story begins at Shorecrest High School in Seattle, where she was a three-time All-American (national select team). However, she almost didn't make it that far as football (or soccer) was not her first love. When Michelle was a little girl, her dream was to play wide receiver for the Pittsburgh Steelers. She practised making catches in the back garden every day with her father and brother, but then a well-meaning teacher took little Michelle aside and told her the cold, hard truth: 'Girls don't play [American] football!'

Even when she turned her attention to football/soccer, her first experience was not a happy one:

> They put me in goal, because I was the only one who would go after the ball, and fight for the ball, and dive in the mud, 'cause I thought that was the best thing in the world, until we were losing like 10–0. So after every game, I cried and cried, and hated soccer. I begged my mom, 'Please, let me stop playing. I hate it, I hate it,' but really the reason I hated it was because we kept losing, and I wanted to win. But my mom said, 'No, you've got to finish out the season.'

So she did – and things got better!

Away from football, life was not without its problems. Michelle's parents split up when she was 10 and that day is an indelible memory for her: 'It was really hard. I can remember watching my dad leave. He had a pillow underneath his arm and it was raining, and it was dark. And he walked down the steps and I remember looking out the upstairs window and my dad got in the truck and drove away.'

Michelle reacted to her parents' divorce in a way that was understandable, but not really helpful. She started hanging out with some of the bad crowd, partying, making wrong decisions, skipping school and generally started going off on the wrong track.

Eventually, she got to the point where she was tired of

fighting it, tired of being scared, tired of messing everything up, and was tired of being lost.

One particular teacher proved to be a great influence just when she needed it. His name was Al Kovats, the high school English teacher:

> One day I asked him, 'What's your deal?' He said, 'Well, I'm a Christian.' And he said, 'Do you know what that is?' And I thought I did. I had grown up going to church, and I said, 'Oh yeah, I go to church – God and all that junk.' He said, 'No, no – it's a relationship with Jesus.'
>
> And so he started telling me all about it. And I was, like, 'Well, that's nice, but that ain't for me. If I become a Christian, that means I have to stand apart from the crowd; I'll probably have to get some nun outfit and I'll be a nerd, and there's no way I can do it.' But finally, after the course of a year of our friendship deepening, and he was able to share more things with me, I came to the end of my rope. And he was driving home from basketball practice one night, and we're sitting in the driveway, in the dark and rain, and I was crying. I said, 'I just can't take it. I hate what I'm doing. I'm scared, and I want to know this Jesus.'

After high school, Michelle became a student at the University of Central Florida in Orlando, where she became all-time leading scorer in UCF history and a member of the school's Hall of Fame. At UCF she was a four-time All-American, Central Florida's Athlete of the Year in 1988–9, and Most Valuable Attacking Player at the 1987 NCAA Final Four. When she left, UCF retired the number 10 jersey that she had worn.

The problem was that Michelle started to believe her own press: 'I was playing great, and getting all of this press coverage. It's like I had a constant smile on the inside. I was thinking, "Wow, this is fun!" I was having too much fun to be a Christian.

Essentially I put Jesus in my back pocket and said, "I'm doing this stuff, it's more fun." So I had a good time partying and enjoying myself.'

The problem came when the partying started to get in the way of her performance. Her coach read the riot act to her, and told her she had to make some decisions, and to change her attitude, if she wanted to succeed at university in her studies and her sport. In fact, she had to stay in college for the summer and go to summer school, just to get her grades' average back up.

The date of 18 August 1985 is a red-letter one in the history of Women's Football in America. The USA played its first-ever game, against Italy, in Italy. Three days later, the USA drew 2–2 with Denmark in the tournament in Italy, with Michelle scoring the first-ever goal for the USA in international football.

Over the next five years she played regularly for the US team, and by the end of 1990 had scored 15 goals in 24 games. The year 1991 saw both her and her game move up a gear, when the first-ever Women's Football World Cup was played in China.

The USA began with a 3–2 win over Sweden, before beating Brazil 5–0 and Japan 3–0, to progress to the quarter-final. They crushed Chinese Taipei (Taiwan) 7–0, with Michelle scoring five goals.

A 5–2 win over Germany put them in the final to play Norway, who beat Sweden in the other semi. The USA became the first World Cup winners by beating Norway 2–1 in the final, with Michelle scoring both goals for a tally of 10 in the competition. As well as the Golden Boot Award – as leading goal scorer – she also won the Silver Ball Award as the second best player in the tournament. Therefore 1991 was, overall, a quite phenomenal year, with 39 goals in 26 games.

After the World Cup, life went mad – a frenzy of appearances to promote the women's game, the endorsements and the media, and all that went with it. When Michelle resumed training it was a struggle: 'I couldn't get going. And I was tired. I wasn't sleeping good, I had bad headaches. Usually I'm just revved, can't wait to get in training. Now, when I stepped on the field, it was an effort to tie my shoes. So I knew something was going on, but I thought it was the effects of the World Cup maybe.'

In fact, it was the start of a struggle with an illness later to be diagnosed as Chronic Fatigue Immune Dysfunction Syndrome (CFIDS). In 1996, Michelle was asked to testify before Congress for CFIDS Awareness Day and this is part of her written testimony:

It wasn't long after the World Cup [1991] that I began to notice a change in my energy. Over a two-year period, almost imperceptibly at first, I began to fade. Finally, I collapsed and became delirious on the field during the 1993 Olympic Sports Festival. The doctors thought at first that it might be muscle glycogen depletion, then a heart dysfunction, and finally Epstein-Barr Virus. My numbers were sky high. Bingo! We found the culprit. Or so I thought. I was diagnosed with Chronic Fatigue Immune Dysfunction Syndrome (CFIDS). In 1994, three years later, I finally had a name to the thing I had to fight to regain my health.

I have always believed that you can accomplish anything through hard work and perseverance, through dedication and commitment. This is how I became a world champion and Olympic athlete. That is the irony of the illness. The harder you work, the more it drags you down, the more it disables you. It is the first time in my life I have been beaten. For the first time in my life I may have to quit before I accomplish my goal. I cannot defeat this illness by hard work or pure drive and desire. It is the first time I cannot overcome on my own terms, in my own strength (Testimony to Congress, written on 11 May 1996).

Most of the next four years, between the 1991 and 1995 World Cups, were a complete nightmare for Michelle:

> Most of the time I felt extreme fatigue, just bone weary, just dragging myself around. I felt like I had sandbags on my shoulders, bad headaches – grinding, crushing headaches. I couldn't sleep at night. I was having terrible dreams. I was sweating so much that I went through two or three T-shirts a night. I was throwing up a lot, suffering dizziness and muscle aches. Sometimes it just took every ounce of energy to sit up.
>
> The physical ailments, the physical pain and the illness started to take away more and more of my career and my life. I had got married in 1990, and that relationship was falling apart, just as quickly as I was getting sicker and sicker by the day. When finally my husband and I decided to split, that was the death of a dream for me. When I got married, I expected that to last for ever. And for that to fall apart, and my soccer career was falling apart – I was trying to grab the pieces of my life and my career, and who I thought I was, and it was all just blown apart. After a year of trying to battle the virus, and still maintain my career and marriage, I hit rock bottom emotionally, physically and spiritually.
>
> By 1994, I was just barely playing five, 10 minutes a match. I still scored goals when I got in there – and I was dangerous, if you believe it, for only 10 minutes. Then I'd come out and I'd pay for that 10 minutes for a couple of days, by being in bed and having migraines, just sheer pain.

Michelle's family has a cabin, in the mountains above Seattle where she grew up. At a particularly low point, she decided to go to the cabin for a few days:

> It's a place that I love, because the mountains just surround me and make me feel like nothing. And it's a place that is

quiet, it's a place where no one is going to bother me, and I'm not going to get distracted. I knew I needed to be in that place to get my thoughts together, to look at my life. I wanted to try to figure out what was going on, and try to do something about it. Well, I went there for two weeks and everyone left me alone. I tried to go on walks, and I tried to go hiking. I tried to be outside – and I couldn't be, because I was so sick. So what I ended up doing was just spending time in the cabin, lying on the couch, thinking.

Her thoughts went like this:

OK, here I am. I have achieved my dreams. I have this status. I have this popularity. I have money. I have a home. I have all of these things I've always dreamed of. I have them, and yet they are taken away just like that. And even the stuff that wasn't taken away and I still had, it was no use to me. And so I sat there looking at my little trophies, thinking, 'Um, now what? Now what? I poured out my heart in this one thing, and now I can't play, even for five minutes. So now what will I do? And who am I?'

As we noted earlier, in high school Michelle had put her faith in God, but when she went away to college she had decided she could handle things on her own. Life was good: she'd had a full college scholarship, success in her career, friends, travel, money, husband. 'For 10 years I had lived as I pleased, following my own rules – my own desires. Now I was depressed, sick, alone, and empty. My illness forced me to take a close look at what really mattered in life, what was really true, and who I could really count on.'

When she went to the cabin in the mountains, it had been a long time since she had thought about God, or looked at a Bible, or thought about going to church. But, at rock bottom, she felt she couldn't cope any more:

And so I kind of just said, 'OK, God. You know I can't do it any more. I give up. My life is a mess. But you can have me. Whatever I have left, you can have.'

And from that moment, it wasn't like I knew I was going to be well again, it wasn't like my career came back and everything was hunky-dory, but I kind of knew if I put one foot in front of the other, I was going to make it. I realised that God had made me and that, from the beginning of time, God already had in mind for me who I was, how he was going to put me together, and what my life would be. He had a specific plan for me.

My decision to hand my life over to Jesus brought me incredible peace and strength and joy. Now I know my life is in the hands of someone who loves me and knows what is best for me. God gives me the strength and courage I need to live for him.

Michelle went home from the cabin filled with hope, but still as sick as a dog. She started going to church every week, and then started reading the Bible; and it was a lot of work, and it took a lot of discipline, just like the hard work she was used to as a player:

That's where I found out that it's really discipline, and faith is not necessarily acting on a feeling, but it's saying, 'OK, here's what God says. He has his promise for me, and I can choose to make it real.' So I would daily try to choose, almost minute by minute, choose this hope, choose this strength and grab on. God had it waiting for me, and once I did that, and started exercising these promises, and this faith, I started to understand. That's what it's all about. And my faith started to become real, and going up into the 1995 World Cup, this was the whole focus of my being.

Not that preparation for the World Cup was easy. On a good day, Michelle could get through a practice with the team, but her performance level was not what it had been, and the effort completely wiped her out. On a bad day, she didn't have the strength to get out of bed or shower or fix her own meals. The strain of coping with the disease took its toll on every aspect of her life. It was devastating.

Two entries from her journal at this time sum up how she was thinking:

Having CFIDS has been the most frustrating, depressing experience of my life. By far, this is the toughest thing I have ever fought. The recovery process is long and tedious and requires positive thinking and the utmost patience – which is not a strong trait for me. There have been days when I wanted to die or just give up because of the headaches, fatigue and fevers. (5 July 1995)

I was once what you call a low-maintenance person. No special attention or needs. Independent, strong. But now I need all these special considerations, excuses, rules to live or do the things I want to do. I am high-maintenance. Fragile. For example, to play for the national team is tough. Sometimes I can practise and sometimes not. That's not very reliable. I hate getting sympathy for feeling awful, yet I want people to understand how badly I feel and that I am not just copping out. (3 April 1996)

It was a battle, but Michelle made it to the 1995 World Cup in Sweden – where she had played professional football for three seasons. She made an immediate impact, but not quite in the way she had hoped. The USA's opening game was against China, but Michelle only lasted seven minutes:

As the whistle goes to start the first game of the 1995 World Cup, I'm thinking, 'I made it! I'm in the game!

I fought my way.' Then, a few minutes into the game, I get smashed in the head by a Chinese girl. I was unconscious, fell to the ground crumpled in a heap, and I ripped my medial cruciate ligament. I'm out for the tournament, essentially. So I'm waking up from my concussion a couple of days later, finally coherent, thinking, 'Hmm, this is interesting.' And now I'm really starting to understand what's real in my life. You know I've gone through all of these circumstances before. I kind of had almost been using my faith as a way of getting what I wanted still – and I still wanted my soccer. And the World Cup experience, of being knocked out in that first game, was the beginning of owning my faith.

The USA drew 3–3 with China, but wins over Denmark and Australia saw them meet and beat Japan in the quarter-final. Amazingly, Michelle returned for the semi-final, which was lost 0–1 to Norway, who went on to win the Cup.

The next big event on the horizon was the Olympic Games of 1996 in the USA. For the first time, women's football was to be an Olympic sport. In 1993 Michelle had met one of the top people in the US Olympic Committee and thanked him for the committee's decision to include women's football in the 1996 Olympics Games. He laughed and told her that the committee didn't feel that it had had any choice, after all the letters and petitions they had received as a result of their campaign.

In late 1995 it looked as if the Olympic dream might never materialise. Michelle, and eight team-mates, got into a dispute with the US Soccer Federation. The Federation's compensation proposals required the team to win gold to qualify for a bonus, but the team felt there should also be some recognition for reaching the final, or even the semis. The Federation's initial reaction was 'take it or leave it', and promptly dropped the nine players from the squad, announcing that the players were on strike. Fortunately, the dispute was resolved.

Coach DiCicco's analysis of the defeat in the 1995 World Cup led him to a belief that there was a weakness in midfield. He needed a player who could dominate midfield and distribute the ball well, and he had just the player in mind. On tour in Brazil, he told Michelle he would like to try her in a new role. Having been used to playing as an out-and-out striker all her career, Michelle was not enthusiastic about the change. She felt, too, that she was being taken out of the action, and saw it almost as a demotion. The aim of the game was to score goals, and *her* role in the team had always been to score goals. She was a natural finisher, so the idea of strolling around in midfield did not appeal!

The coach pressed his case. As a target man, Michelle was receiving the ball with her back to goal and was often clattered from behind and picking up a lot of injuries. The coach argued that she would make a bigger contribution in midfield. Then he played what proved to be his trump card! He said that the positional switch could extend her career. If the other arguments did not impress Michelle, the idea of extending her career appealed!

She played in midfield in the South American tour, and then in a home game with Norway, the reigning world champions, in Tampa. The USA won 3–2, with coach DiCicco saying, 'She had an awesome game. The Norwegians simply didn't know how to deal with her. She would take the ball, escape pressure and change the point of attack more quickly than we had ever been able to do against Norway before.' The switch to midfield had been made. Full speed ahead to the Olympics!

However, with Michelle things are never that simple! Early in 1996 she injured her knee in a warm-up before a game in Jacksonville. The team doctor told her that, for the second time in two years, her medial cruciate ligament was badly torn, and that surgery was needed. However, with the Olympics five months and 17 days away, there was not time for surgery and rehabilitation.

In the midst of the crisis, humour struck. Michelle wanted to speak to her manager and left the locker room to find a payphone. In fact, she had to leave the stadium to find one. Then, as she made her way back, in her US team tracksuit, signing autographs for fans, she had a problem. Security would not let her back in!

It has to be said that the humour is greater in retrospect. At the time, standing outside the stadium, 'in full uniform, crying, my Olympic dream shattered, arguing with Security, unable to get inside the stadium', it seemed anything but funny.

A second medical opinion was more encouraging: she would have two to three hours of physiotherapy a day on the knee to see if the injury would respond. By 20 April, the recovery had gone so well that she was in the starting line-up against Holland. She played OK, scored and, more importantly, lasted 90 minutes unscathed. This was followed by playing – and scoring – in part of two more friendlies that month.

A consultation with a CFIDS specialist led to a strict 10-week elimination diet – no dairy products, no caffeine, no red meat, no gluten, no sugar – or, as Michelle put it, 'No more TCBY [frozen yoghurt], no Cinnabons, pizza or my beloved Starbuck's. I began living on gluten-free cereal, Powerbars, dried gluten-free soups, gluten-free bread, rice-milk, popcorn, gluten-free pancake mix, corn or rice pastas, peanut butter and carrots.' At times, though, it seemed as if she was surviving on carrot juice and Powerbars.

In May, the USA played in a tournament, beating Japan 4–0, China 1–0 and Canada 6–0. Against China, Michelle picked up a loose ball 30 yards from goal and scored the winner.

Those three wins increased the sense of anticipation about the Olympics on home soil and the first-ever women's Olympic football tournament. If it went well it would be a springboard for women's football.

On 18 July the team travelled by chartered bus from their training centre in Sanford, Florida to the Olympic village at Michelle's alma mater, the University of Central Florida, escorted by motorcycle cops and police cruisers with sirens wailing and lights flashing. Traffic parted like the Red Sea. The city of Orlando, an Olympic venue for football only, and Michelle's adopted home city, was a very welcoming base.

Michelle's team-mates then flew to Atlanta for the opening ceremony. Michelle herself did not go, to preserve her energy. She had planned to watch the opening ceremony, but was asleep by 10 p.m!

At last the action started. The USA played Denmark in the opening game, watched by 25,303 people, by far the largest ever US crowd for women's football. Michelle says, 'The Citrus Bowl rocked! Add to all that, the Olympic theme and the national anthem . . . and whoa! When we walked out in our white jerseys to the Olympic theme I was barely holding it together. We're talking goose bumps and a major lump in the throat! That moment was awesome. I looked for Dad in the audience and gave him the usual thumbs up.'

As Denmark prepared to make a goal kick, Michelle told Mia Hamm that if the kick landed anywhere near Michelle, Mia should make a run and Michelle would aim to put the ball in a space ahead of her. The plan worked to perfection. The goal kick came to Michelle and she planted her header in space for Hamm to time her run perfectly for the first goal.

With the USA 3–0 up, DiCicco subbed Michelle after 76 minutes. She came off to a standing ovation and told the media, 'I had a blast out there!' After each game Steve Slain, the fitness coach, was responsible for getting Michelle to the locker room as quickly as possible where Mark Adams would set her up on IV to aid her recovery.

The second game against Sweden was tougher than expected. With 16 minutes left, the USA led, but only 1–0. When Shannon MacMillan put the USA two goals ahead, the game seemed over, but two minutes later Sweden scored. While the plan had been to sub Michelle before the end, the tightness of the game required her to stay on the pitch until the end.

Shortly after the final whistle, a team-mate took a picture of Michelle – ice-bag on her head, ice-bag on her thigh, two ice-bags on her knee and ankle, hand and toe taped and hooked up to IV. Fortunately, Michelle saw the funny side too. On another occasion one of the trainers told her that half the Soccer Federation's budget went on tape for her!

The USA met China in the group decider in Miami, in front of 43,525 fans. For a game that produced 26 attempts on goal, 0–0 was an unlikely score. With the USA having 19 of the efforts, they were disappointed not to have made their chances count. However, as the draw saw both teams through to the semi-finals, nothing was lost for either team by the stalemate. Near the end of the game, Michelle heard her brother, who was near the touch-line, yell, 'Dig deep!' She remembers thinking, 'I'm already giving it everything I have; there's nothing more.' Then she tried to find some more!

After reaching the last four the team flew to Atlanta, as the remaining games were to be in Athens, Georgia. Michelle was playing every game, making a contribution, but it was a battle:

My symptoms and weariness grew more severe after every game. I was running out of gas earlier during the matches, and finding it harder to recover afterwards. Injuries were taking their toll as well. My right knee had to be drained before the semi-final. My big toe still needed to be taped. My hand was taped because of a sprained thumb and finger.

I remember thinking, 'This knee is flopping all over like spaghetti, not sure how long that thing is going to hold up.' And then, 'Here I am in the Olympics, going for a gold medal!' It was really a situation where I shouldn't have been able to compete. Before a game I would pray, in my locker room, with my head bowed: 'OK, God, I'm just willing to go wherever you take me. If I can't last, I know you're going to use it. Give me the grace and the strength to endure sitting on the sidelines and watching my team participate in these Olympics that I so badly want to compete in.' And so every game I would step on the field, not knowing if I was going to make it.

Michelle had played as a striker in the first three games. For the semi against Norway, coach DiCicco would play her in midfield. He had deliberately kept the switch until now, to surprise the Norwegians.

Some 64,000 attended the game at Sanford Stadium, University of Georgia, and DiCicco was delighted with Michelle's performance: 'She really surprised Norway. They had no answer for her. She won every head-ball that came near her.' Michelle's dominance of the high balls thwarted Norway's tactics of setting up their attack with long balls out of defence. DiCicco continued:

We had 28 attempts on goal against Norway in that game, which is unheard of, because they are such a great defensive team. We did it because Michelle was spraying the ball around very much like a great quarterback, hitting receivers all over the field. Her technical speed – the ability to receive a ball, prepare it and play it somewhere – was so fast. And her skill at serving balls with the inside or the outside of either foot is the best I've ever seen from any player, man or woman. She proved that to me again in that game.

While the USA were playing well, a defensive error midway through the first half gave Norway a chance to score the opening goal. At half-time Michelle told the coaches, 'I can't keep going, I can't do it. I'm outta gas.' Steve Slain replied, 'You will finish. You've gotta finish.'

With 80 minutes gone, Norway still led 1–0. The Olympic dream seemed decidedly rocky, but then there was a handball by a Norwegian defender: penalty. Michelle takes up the story:

The second I realised we were being awarded a penalty kick, I wanted it. I looked around to see who else wanted it. Carla was off getting water. Brandi was standing in the back; she was out. I looked at Tony, and he pointed at me. 'Rock on!' I thought.

Stepping up to the mark, I took the ball from the official. I thought to myself, this is the moment I've been waiting for, all my life. I was calm. I was confident. And very aware of the importance of this kick. If we miss, we'll probably lose and there will be no gold medal. I decided to go to the left and drive it so hard that if the keeper did get a hand on the ball, it would take her right into the net. I looked to the right and then focused only on the ball during my approach. I felt no doubt.

GOAL!

Before the game, coach DiCicco had nominated his penalty takers – Michelle was second or third on the list. He says:

> But when the foul was called, only one person turned and looked at me. And the assertiveness with which Michelle stared towards the bench communicated loud and clear. She was asking, 'Who do you want to take this?' But her body language said, 'It had better be me!' So I just pointed to her. Because that is what I like to see, as a coach – somebody who wants to take that critical shot in such a pressure situation.

Full-time came: 1–1. Everyone gathered around the DiCicco for instructions prior to extra time. Michelle lay flat on her back in the middle of the huddle: 'And as I looked up at my team-mates stacking hands above me, I prayed for the strength to carry on a few more minutes. Steve Slain pulled me to my feet, smacked me on the butt, and told me to get out and do it.'

Extra time was under the golden goal rule – the first goal would win the game. The USA got it. After 10 minutes, Shannon MacMillan, who had just come on as a sub, took a pass from Julie Foudy, and scored. The USA were in the Olympic final! Michelle was helped back to the locker room, then she was told she had to go to the press conference. It was up four flights of stairs and they almost had to carry her!

On 1 August 1996 a crowd of 76,481 gathered at Sanford Stadium for the final – the largest crowd ever to attend a women's sports event. The final was against China, the one team the USA had not managed to beat in the Olympic competition. Michelle again played a midfield role, her task being to win balls and distribute them.

In the eighteenth minute Tiffeny Milbrett carried the ball forward, before laying it off to Michelle. She found Kristine Lilly on the left wing. Mia Hamm met Lilly's cross, and goal-keeper Gao Hong parried the shot on to the post. Shannon MacMillan was there to slot the rebound home. However, China equalised before half-time.

One of Steve Slain's assignments during the Games was to assess Michelle's survival and to advise coach DiCicco if he felt she needed to be subbed. During the final he knew Michelle would not want to come off before the end, so at one point he threw her a Powerbar and told her to carry on. There is a great picture of Michelle winning a tackle with a half-eaten Powerbar in her hand. As one of her family said, 'Just like Popeye and his spinach!'

After 72 minutes, Mia Hamm broke on the right, fed Joy Fawcett, who found Millie (Tiffeny Milbrett) – Goal! The last 18 minutes seemed to last for ever, then finally the whistle blew. Michelle and her team were Olympic champions! What does that moment feel like?

Standing there on the podium was a moment I had dreamed of for years, and now it was real. I stood there trying to soak up every feeling, image and thought, wanting to immortalise and memorise this once-in-a-lifetime moment. It's everything you can imagine. Almost surreal; extremely emotional. Tears, laughter, disbelief, joy – all at once. And all very overwhelming. 'Christ must really be in me,' I thought – because a year ago – injured in the World Cup with a concussion – I was sick and distraught, but now I was standing on this podium with a gold medal round my neck and I felt the same peace inside.

Michelle wrote in her journal the day after the final:

My thoughts are scattered and disjointed, but the sentiment and unforgettable memories will forever be embedded in my heart. My mind keeps returning to the past few years when I thought I was so alone, so isolated in my struggles and pain. God is so good. Through it all, he was preparing me for this moment, this experience. He is so faithful. He took it all away, but he gave me back so much more. I go to bed tonight an Olympic Champion! (2 August 1996)

Michelle took a break from the national team after the Olympics final on 1 August 1996 to recover from knee surgery and chronic fatigue syndrome, and did not play a full international game for the USA until October 1997, against Sweden.

In 1999 the Olympic champions sought to regain the World Cup. They started with comfortable wins over Denmark, Nigeria and Korea, then they beat Germany in the quarter-final and Brazil 2–0 in the semi-final, with Michelle scoring. In the final they met their old adversaries, China. There was nothing between the teams. Half-time: 0–0. Full-time: 0–0. After extra time: 0–0. Penalty shoot-out: USA 5 China 4. However, Michelle didn't make it to the end – she was injured and stretchered off after a collision. Team doctors had to cut off her match shirt in the locker room:

All I remember was lying in the foetal position in a Rose Bowl exam room, while they snipped off my jersey and attached me to two IVs, an oxygen mask and an EKG machine.

I'll never know how I made it to the podium for the trophy presentation, but I'm glad I did. Standing there with the team was such an intense moment, and so was the scene afterwards when I wobbled off the stage and the crowd started chanting, 'Akers! Akers! Akers!' I was blown away! To be acknowledged like that was one of the most incredible gifts of my career.

After the World Cup win, the victorious team went on a coast-to-coast celebration tour – from a Disneyland parade to the New York City talk shows, to a White House visit to a space shuttle launch in Florida. But Michelle was so physically spent that there was no way she could have handled the demands of such a trip, so she stayed home and chilled out.

The year 1999 had been an amazing one. In January, when Michelle scored against Portugal, it was her hundredth international goal. In the World Cup she earned a winner's medal, as well as the Bronze Ball as the third most valuable player, and was named in the 1999 Women's World Cup All-Star Team. Overall in 1999, she played in 20 matches for the USA, starting 18, and scoring six goals.

Michelle had planned to bring down the curtain on her illustrious career after the 2000 Olympics in Sydney. In 2000 she played seven times for the USA – although she only started in three of those.

However, by the end of the Atlanta Olympics, Michelle had made a significant decision:

After winning the gold medal in 1996, I promised myself to never again play in the condition I was in during those Olympic Games. Since then, retirement has been a big issue with me, and the decision to continue with the national team has always been a prayerful and careful one.

After the 1999 World Cup, I wrestled for months about whether to play or not, but eventually decided to go for it, because I knew that unless I was absolutely sure I had spent every possible ounce of myself trying to play, I would beat myself up with second-guessing for the rest of my life.

Then in mid-August – one month before the start of the Sydney Olympics – as she struggled with a shoulder injury, she knew the game was up. She issued a statement that she was withdrawing from the squad:

After battling back from a messed-up shoulder and making the Olympic Team, I found myself at the end – physically and mentally – with a body ready for a M★A★S★H unit. It has been a hard-fought year.

The shoulder injury has definitely been one of the toughest ever. Not only because of the physical pain, the surgery, and the rehabilitation, but because of the mental anguish that goes along with trying to come back in a short time-frame to make the Olympic team. Then having to deal with setback after setback and complication after complication, all the while knowing that every day and every hour counts, as to whether you will make it back in time or not.

This year just seems to have been a non-stop climb of Mount Everest, with 80-mile gale winds in my face. But even in saying that, I know that to climb a mountain, one only needs to put one foot in front of the other and, hopefully, if you do that long enough, you eventually reach the summit. That's how it has been in years past for me, and that's how I fully expected it to be this year. I knew it would be tough and I knew I would want to quit at times, but I have always been able to find something from somewhere to pull me through. Unfortunately though, things did not relent, and instead of catching a much-needed break, as in the past, this time things only got tougher.

I finally said to myself, 'This is insane.' I was taking IVs like Gatorade, and getting injections and taking meds for pain. Ice-packs and tape were a part of my wardrobe! I was battling at my absolute gut level to just get through the day, and finally, the last straw was that I re-injured the shoulder. Finally, I just said, enough is enough. I am no good to myself like this, and I am certainly no good to my team. The decision not to go to Sydney was just as agonising, but I have huge peace in knowing I fought to the very end and have nothing else to give.

Asked when she feels she was at her absolute peak as a player, Michelle Akers has two answers. The simple one is: 'As an athlete, I can tell you I peaked in '91, before my illness took hold of me. After that, I was merely trying to survive.'

But as she reflects more on her career, she sees how the illness and her physical limitations led her to positional changes which represented peaks in their own right:

I think I got 'good' in 1990, and from then on stayed at a very high level of performance, despite injury and illness. After I got sick and was moved from striker to central midfield or withdrawn striker, or even defensive midfield, I was still scoring goals.

I also had the responsibility to play-make and organise and play defence. By '99, and much to my surprise and delight, I had evolved into a pretty good defender. So to answer the question 'when I peaked' is a tough one. My role on the field changed two or three times during my career, and with each change I got 'good' in a different capacity.

After retiring, Michelle began training to be a paramedic, but her injuries have put that on hold for now. She needs another knee reconstruction and still suffers with a bad shoulder (an injury inflicted by a fan who grabbed her after a game in the 1999 World Cup). After surgery she will see how it has healed, and decide whether to continue to pursue the paramedic training. She also has three horses and has been 'really enjoying riding and doing cowgirl stuff'. She does soccer camps in the summer (in Orlando and Seattle) and continues to help out with the University of Central Florida women's soccer programme.

In 2000, Michelle was named as Women's Player of the Century by the world governing body, FIFA. It was an amazing accolade in recognition of her outstanding contribution to the game. Double World Cup winner, FIFA Player of the Century, Olympic gold medallist. It is fitting to end this chapter with the words she expressed just after that 1996 Olympic triumph:

The Olympic Games are also about conquering obstacles. It's about incredible passion, fire, desire. It is about becoming more than you are. By reaching for our dreams, we inspire others to reach for theirs.

My mind keeps returning to the past few years when I thought I was so alone, so isolated in my struggles and pain. God is so good. Through it all, he was preparing me for this moment, this experience. So faithful! He took it all away, but he gave me back so much more.

And that gold medal is just a brief moment, a tangible sign that I can trust God. I can trust him with the thing I care about most, my passion of my life – I can trust him with that. And also it's not enough. It's not enough. That gold medal is not enough. But it's a symbol of what is enough. He brought me to a crossroads where I had to choose – soccer or him. And I chose him, but he gave me my soccer as well.

Olympic record

1996
Gold

This chapter draws on Michelle's autobiography The Game and the Glory: An Autobiography, *by Michelle Akers with Gregg Lewis (Zondervan, 2000), and is supplemented by personal conversations and e-mail exchanges with her.*

8

Jonathan Edwards, an Olympic Odyssey

Jonathan Edwards has competed in four Olympics, but ironically his greatest triumph came in none of them. It was in the 1995 World Championships that Jonathan broke the world record and the 18-metre barrier – not once, but twice.

Now the World Championships themselves have to be seen as just the culmination of an incredible year in 1995. At the start of the 1995 season, Jonathan was a good, international class triple-jumper, but who cared then about the triple jump? By the end of the season, he was an international superstar and had put the triple jump firmly on the map.

In 1989 he cleared 17 metres for the first time, but by the end of 1994 his personal best had only progressed to 17.44 metres. Then came 1995, when Jonathan competed 14 times and won 14 times. He broke the world record three times and had another jump denied world-record status because of the strength of the wind.

On a night in Göteborg, Sweden, in August 1995 Jonathan took the World Championships triple jump by storm by breaking the world record with a jump of 18.16 metres, and then breaking it again with a leap of 18.29 metres. In all, he did four legal jumps (plus three with illegal wind levels) in excess of 18 metres in 1995.

Could he explain why 1995 was so much better than 1994 or 1993? 'Not really. I was running faster, I was stronger, I improved my technique but it still did not add up to what happened. Obviously I wasn't in touch with what my potential was, as it was still a big surprise to me. I look back and shake my head. The other thing to cope with as well is that I had broken through a barrier, the 18-metre triple jump.'

It is strange how in sport there is often a kind of glass ceiling – for some 35 years the standard in the triple jump has been 17 point something metres. This is what triple-jumpers do – they jump 17 metres. Like the four-minute mile, the 18-metre triple jump is a goal to be shot for. Then suddenly an athlete – Jonathan – jumps 18 metres and the whole ball-game changes.

However, if Jonathan thought that winning the world title and breaking the world record would relieve the pressure, he was wrong! Every time he jumped, people expected him to jump 18 metres, if not break the world record.

Jonathan grew up the son of a vicar in Devon and he traces his own faith back to childhood:

I haven't got a day or a date when I became a 'born-again Christian'. It was very much a natural progression just from the reality of God in my Mum's and Dad's lives. I matured and grew as a Christian at home, but I look at the time when I left home. So strong was the influence of my home that it wasn't until I had left and found my own feet – my own spiritual feet, if you like – that I saw the most growth in my own Christian life. I have never not known God, although I realise I haven't always been a Christian. But God has always been there.

Jonathan was good at sport through school and university, but never really seemed a potential world champion. After leaving university he found a job in Newcastle and joined Gateshead Harriers. He was selected for the 1988 Olympics – but almost wasn't.

The system for selection was that the first two in the UK Olympic trials were guaranteed selection, with a third place at the discretion of the selectors. However, the trials were scheduled for a Sunday and Jonathan decided not to take part for that reason. He felt then, as a Christian, that he should not compete on the Lord's Day. Fortunately, there was a happy ending as the selectors chose him anyway, along with the two from the trials, and he was on his way to Korea.

At that time Jonathan's personal best was 16.74 metres, which he had set just a month before the Olympics. Sadly, in Seoul, he failed to do himself justice, jumping only 15.88 metres and failing to qualify for the second stage. The competition was won by Khristo Markov of Bulgaria with 17.61 metres. Had Jonathan equalled his personal best, he would have finished in eighth place.

His recollections of 1988 are: 'A great deal of fun. It was also my introduction into international athletics. Just being part of the whole Olympic set-up and meeting lots of famous people, from the point of view of an athlete.' He recalls being overawed at the whole thing, and the excitement of meeting Daley Thompson. He felt like 'the new kid on the team, watching, learning, finding his feet'.

Also, with regard to his Christian life it was a very exciting time. Kriss Akabusi was on the team, and Barrington Williams and Vernon Samuels. The Christians were meeting regularly together. There was a kind of spontaneity, and it was the start of the Christians in Sport in Athletics movement. So from two points of view, athletically and spiritually, it was very exciting with lots of new things happening.

Athletically, Jonathan set himself a target. It was fine to enjoy the Olympic experience and the exhilaration of being part of the greatest sporting show on earth, but next time he wanted to come back with the chance of competing for a medal and not be an also-ran.

By the time the Barcelona Olympics came along, Jonathan had progressed up the world rankings and was a serious medal contender. However, he began to feel the weight of expectations; he was, quite simply, a man expected to deliver.

When Jonathan set a new personal best of 17.43 metres in Carlisle in June 1991, it was a distance that put him into the world-class level. It would have taken bronze in the 1988 Olympics (and, for that matter, in 1992), so Jonathan had every justification in heading for Barcelona with expectations of a medal.

There was one anxious moment in his preparation. When he read in the Olympic schedule that the event-qualifying stage was on a Saturday, he feared the worst – the triple-jump final would be on the Sunday. However, he was relieved to find that Sunday was a rest day, with the final on the Monday. Jonathan gave thanks to God.

With the Olympics in Europe, the family were going to be part of it, and his parents, brother Tim, with wife Anna, had driven to Spain. Jonathan's wife, Alison, was flying in to join them on the evening of 1 August, the day of the qualifying competition.

The qualifying competition, which should have been a formality, proved to be an unmitigated disaster for Jonathan. He had three jumps to secure his place in the final. On the first he lost his run-up and ran through the sandpit. His other two jumps were 15.76 and 15.06 metres. He had failed to make the final, when he certainly had the potential to win a medal.

This is his own account of the 1992 Olympics:

Any athlete will tell you that the run-up to major games are fraught with little niggling injuries and nagging doubts, yet, as I recall my lead-in to Barcelona, my only thought is that I couldn't have wished for better. Physically I was in excellent shape, and spiritually I was aware of God's hand on me in a very real way, and I felt strong confirmation that God wanted me to be an athlete. I honestly felt that it was God's will for me to succeed, whatever that entailed.

As Linford Christie fulfilled his Olympic dream, mine came to an unheralded end. I don't think I have ever felt such pain and anguish. It had to be a bad dream: I would wake up any minute and do it for real – anything to give relief from the reality. Could I have heard God so wrongly? Could I carry on as an athlete? I was frightened too – my whole future, and my wife Alison's, also seemed blown apart in just three awful jumps.

I honestly thought it must be a bad dream. It was a profound experience. You can be upset and disappointed but think there is always another day. But this went to the core of me. It got to me in a way I probably didn't anticipate much could.

I went into the competition thinking I had a chance of winning a medal, and then it all went very horribly wrong. I didn't even make 16 metres, and I had been jumping 17 metres reasonably consistently throughout the season. It was probably the worst period of my life athletically and I was absolutely devastated. All my hopes and dreams had been blown out of the water. I remember going to bed in the evening thinking, I'll wake up in the morning and it will all be a dream; this isn't reality; it can't have happened. This wasn't the way it was supposed to happen. It was awful. There is no other way of describing it. I was taken to depths that I had not known previously.

Meeting Alison after those jumps was both a relief and a nightmare. It was great to be with family, yet Alison's reaction seemed to say, 'What have we been doing all these years?' The next day, Jonathan had a conversation with Kriss Akabusi, who was in his own last Olympics. As they talked, it became clear that Jonathan would take on some of Kriss's role within the group of Christian athletes in the team, and that helped to give some meaning and hope for the future.

After the Olympics it was back to business. One encouraging aspect was that the season was far from over and there were still opportunities to show what might have happened in Barcelona. In reality, over the next weeks as he strove to regain his form, things only got worse. From jumping 17-plus metres consistently, 16-plus metres became a real difficulty. His self-confidence was shattered:

A lot of the time I was numb to it all, but sometimes the reality of what was happening would break through, and in those times the pain was almost too much to bear. Within athletics I felt talentless, uninteresting, insignificant, and I often just wanted to run away during competitions because I couldn't bear the humiliation.

During all this I never felt that God was far away. I didn't understand, but I knew that God was working out his ways for good. Like the Psalmist, I asked, 'Why are you downcast, O my Soul? Put your hope in God for I will yet praise him, my Saviour and my God.' I was learning again that my hope was to be in God and not in happy circumstances, and that, come what may, he is worthy to be praised. And in my heart God gave me an assurance that things wouldn't always be like this, and an expectancy that he could turn things around and put wings on my feet at any time and restore my jumping form.

Ironically, the turning point came in Turin, where again he jumped badly, coming eighth with 16.48 metres. However, while waiting to jump, he rediscovered his focus and realised that he was jumping for God! He could be the worst triple-jumper the world has ever seen, but triple jump was what he was going to do! He realised that it wasn't about *him*. If God had called him into athletics, nothing had changed. Suddenly, though, he saw that he had to trust God and not his own ability.

There was only one competition left that season, the IAAF World Cup in Havana, Cuba on 26 September 1992. Jonathan jumped 17.34 metres – and won! 'I was not entirely prepared for Havana, when I finished first in the World Cup triple jump with my third best-ever jump – ironically, enough to have given me fourth place in the Olympics! I can only say that it was a miracle. People will read this and think me simplistic and naïve to say such a thing, but I know it to be true. The God we serve is indeed mighty and I will never forget Havana, or Barcelona, or who it is who gives me my strength.'

As he looks back on a career of four Olympics, World Championships and world records, Jonathan is sure that God has been in it all. Of the 1992 nightmare he now says:

I think God had been disciplining me at those Olympics; not to punish me, but to bring me closer to him. I look back to that now, and other difficult times that I have had, and recognise that they have been fundamental in the growth of my faith and my maturing as a Christian.

I think that, at that stage, it was the first real, real, real crisis I had faced as a Christian, independent from living at home. At that time I thought, 'Do I really believe this? Am I really going to go for it 100 per cent, come what may, win or lose? Is God first? Am I going to glorify him and give my best to him, regardless of results?' From that point of view, it was crucial and laid a foundation for the ensuing years in athletics, and particularly in my spiritual life.

I am much more of the opinion now that I am at the mercy of the ups and downs of life. Sport accentuates the ups and downs – one moment everything is fine, the next it's all fallen apart. I don't doubt that God is involved – but how exactly I don't know. Except to say that God's ultimate ambition is to conform me to the image of Christ. And he will have tried to do that, no doubt, through those various experiences. As for looking for a grand plan – did the failure of Barcelona prepare me for the triumph of Göteborg? – I am not sure.

The period between the 1992 and the 1996 Olympic Games falls neatly into two halves for Jonathan. The years 1993 and 1994 were not bad ones – in the World Championships in 1993 he did a personal best of 17.44 metres to take bronze. In 1994 he had a disappointing sixth place in the European Championships, followed by silver at the Commonwealth Games.

On 27 June 1993 Jonathan competed in the European Cup in Rome on a Sunday – it was his first-ever Sunday competition. In 1991 the two major events of the year had been the World Championships and the European Cup and, in both, the triple jump was scheduled for a Sunday. Jonathan came under a certain amount of pressure – he was told that he was letting his country down by refusing to jump. However, he stuck to his principles and went to church while others competed in the big events of 1991.

Shortly before the 1991 World Championships, Jonathan explained his position: 'As a Christian, God comes first in my life, and keeping Sunday special is not so much following a rigid rule; it is just a way of showing that God is first in my life and not my athletics.'

After the disappointment of 1992, Jonathan needed 1993 to be a good year, but when he learnt that every major competition of 1993 was to be on a Sunday, he was stunned. He was convinced that God was calling him to be an athlete and to be a part of the Christian presence within the British athletics team, and being a witness to his fellow athletes, yet the door was being slammed in his face.

As Jonathan thought and prayed about the issue, he came more clearly to the view that he should jump on Sundays. 'My reason for deciding to compete on Sundays was that I knew that if I did not, I would be opting out of most of the major competitions, so denying myself the opportunity of developing my gift to its full potential in the world of athletics. The basis for that decision was a conviction from my own Bible study that I was now free to do so.'

Then came that incredible year of 1995 – unbeaten and world record holder. Roll on the next Olympics! The year ended with Jonathan receiving a plethora of awards, one of which, in particular, meant a great deal to him – the BBC Sports Personality of the Year: 'It was incredible, simply because it is the British sporting award of the year. There are others which, athletically, mean more, but this is the British public voting for you in a programme that has been on for years and years. You look at the names of those who've won it across all the sports. It was incredible to me. To think of some of the great sportspeople who've never won it – and to think that my name will be there, recorded in history for ever. It's remarkable.'

The year 1996 started well enough: eight competitions and eight wins – taking the winning sequence to 22. His winning distances that he was jumping were in the range of 17.29 to 17.79 metres (wind assisted). If not quite 1995 form, it was a solid enough platform from which to go for gold.

The qualifying stage of the 1996 Olympic triple jump was scheduled for Friday 26 July, and it was later that same evening that a terrorist bomb went off in Centennial Park, Atlanta, killing one person and injuring a further 110.

To qualify for the final, a triple-jumper had to jump 17 metres or come in the top 12. The ideal scenario for a jumper in the qualifiers is to put in a jump of 17 metres at the first attempt, put on one's tracksuit, and go home.

Whether or not it was particularly in his mind that he had failed to qualify for either of the 1988 and 1992 Olympic finals, but Jonathan made heavy weather of this one. His first jump was 16.93 metres. Second jump: 16.96 metres. While he reasoned that it was highly unlikely that 12 other athletes would jump further, and that he would be in the final, he was concerned at his form, which he described as 'pathetic'. He summed up his attitude: 'I was completely demoralised and felt absolutely dreadful.'

By lunchtime the following day – the day of the final – he was a mental wreck. 'I just wanted to get out. I wasn't thinking about winning a gold medal. I was thinking I couldn't jump.' As someone has said, Jonathan is 'a man capable of talking himself into depression after one poor performance'.

Again, it was a spiritual experience that gave him strength. All the competitors had been given a copy of the New Testament with some words on the front cover from the book of 1 Peter, chapter 1, verse 7: 'These trials prove that your faith is worth much more than gold.' The words spoke to Jonathan: 'Of course, I had noticed it before, but this was the time it jumped out at me – ". . . your faith is worth much more than gold, that can be destroyed . . . and you will be given praise and honour and glory when Jesus Christ returns." It put my predicament in perspective and was a great comfort to me. A reassurance, it reaffirmed that this wasn't about me being successful. This was about my walk with God. And I thought, "If I win, I win; and if I don't, I don't." '

Jonathan started with a no-jump. It was good, and would have been about 17.70 metres if he had not overstepped – good for his confidence, if not his score. Afterwards he commented that it would have been a completely different competition had that jump gone in. He would have set his stall out and would have been relaxed, knowing he had made a good start and with five more jumps to go.

Local favourite Kenny Harrison jumped 17.99 metres with his opening attempt, but Jonathan no-jumped again. 'I was down and the referee had reached nine . . . I was praying madly. I was fighting for my survival.'

In Barcelona, while Jonathan struggled, Linford Christie was winning gold. In Atlanta, as Jonathan struggled, Linford was being controversially disqualified for a false start.

With his third jump, Jonathan recorded 17.13 metres, which put him in third place and qualified him for three more jumps.

With his fourth jump, he produced 17.88 metres – 'I don't know where I got 17.88 from but suddenly, Bang! The competition had begun for me.' But in the fifth round, Kenny Harrison jumped 18.09 metres and Jonathan no-jumped again.

Jonathan had one jump left. He felt good, was balanced, and landed well. For the first time in Atlanta, he felt he was running hard and jumping like he had in 1995, but now he had overstepped slightly and it was a no-jump. If it had not been for the overstep, the jump, at about 18.20 metres, would have been enough to win gold – but silver it was, and he was not too disappointed. He felt he had jumped well and had just been beaten by somebody who jumped better on the day, and he feels frustrated that people still ask him about the *failure* at Atlanta.

The irony is that the media know as well as anybody how fickle sport is, especially something like the triple jump. It is a highly technical event – much more so than an event on the track. But, Jonathan feels, for the British media it has to be black and white, whereby it's either great victory or abject failure. Immediately after Atlanta he was delighted with what he had done, delighted with the performance and with the medal.

In 1997 Jonathan was first in the European Cup triple jump and came second in the World Championships, defending his world title. But the year 1998 was an outstanding one. He won the European indoor title, the World Games, the European Championships with a jump of 17.99 metres, the European Cup and the Goodwill Games. The Commonwealth Games were at the end of the season, but sadly injury robbed him of the chance to take part.

In a sequence of 15 events he fouled out once and won the other 14. At the Bislett Games in Oslo, he jumped 18.01 metres, the first 18-metre jump since 1995.

The year 1999 was a harder one, and in the biggest competition of the year, the World Championships in Seville, he came third with 17.48 metres. Afterwards he was seen in tears, hugging Alison. He said later, 'Seville showed me that I did not want to be this hard-hearted athlete. If I cannot win the Olympics without being selfish, I don't want to win.'

But how does that work in practice?

The answer is – with great difficulty. I look back at my athletics career now and think of it as something essentially pretty selfish. I believe it is what God has called me to, and that to a degree it has to be like that. I have to make sure that I get enough sleep and eat the right things. Life revolves around me. I design my life in such a way to ensure that there are as few demands as possible made on me when I am competing. But in many ways, that is the antithesis of the Christian life, which is about self-sacrifice and giving to other people. I have a lot of people giving to me, and with life being tailored to my specifications, quite a childish existence. If I were to stamp my feet and cry, people would come running to see if I were OK.

Such is human nature that it would be easy to take it for granted, and to use it for your own advantage. I am very conscious now as I look forward, and think that I will have to give a lot more of myself to other people. Particularly Alison.

The preparation for Sydney 2000 was all done in the shadow of Alison's mum's terminal illness. Jonathan's form had been good. In 10 competitions he had eight wins, a fourth place and a foul-out. His best jump had been 17.62 metres. Jonathan and his friend Phil Wall had a mantra to describe Sydney: 'Everything – and nothing'. At the same time the Olympics meant everything, and yet nothing at all. His performance in Sydney would define him as an athlete, but not in his more important roles as a man, father and husband.

He arrived in Australia amid a storm of controversy over some comments that had been attributed to him: that swimmers partied too much and were not very professional. Jonathan, though, felt he had been badly misquoted, so he met with British team officials and penned an apology to defuse the situation.

While Jonathan was in the UK training camp along the coast from Sydney, he received the telephone call he had been dreading. Alison's mother had died. It would not be possible for Jonathan to take the 22-hour flight to the UK for the funeral and back to Sydney, without leaving himself so jet-lagged and exhausted that he would not be able to compete. It was one or the other. He felt he was letting Alison down by not being with her in the biggest crisis of her life, and there is no doubt that this added to the pressure on him to win. Put crudely, there was no point in having stayed in Australia if he didn't win gold.

While in the Olympic village, Jonathan was spoken to by an incident in the Bible: the story of the boy who gave his lunch to Jesus, who then used it to feed 5000 people. Like the boy giving the five loaves and two fish to Jesus, Jonathan felt he was being asked to give his triple-jumping to Jesus, for Jesus to make of it what he could. He said later that his prayer was for God to 'give me the strength to cope, come what may. That in victory I don't glorify myself, and in defeat I don't plumb the depths of despair.'

Jonathan safely negotiated this qualifying competition with a jump of 17.08 metres, but he was the third Briton behind Phillips Idowu and Larry Achike. Incidentally, that was the day Steve Redgrave had collected his fifth Olympic gold medal in rowing.

Few people understand the pressure of top-level sport, but Jonathan certainly does: 'Competing at the top level is not fun, it's excruciating. The day and a half between qualifying and the final in Sydney were agony. In Atlanta, I had wanted to go home. You want to be anywhere else in the world and yet you don't, because you're at the top and you've got a real chance of winning. You've also got more to lose.'

The final of the triple jump took place on Monday 25 September. It was the evening that the heroine of all Australia,

Kathy Freeman, was to run in the 400m, and tickets for Stadium Australia were as difficult to come by as hens' teeth. The atmosphere was electric. After Kathy Freeman's win, Michael Johnson took the men's 400m, and then came the triple jump.

When Jonathan started with a legal jump of 17.12 metres, there was a sense of relief. In the second round it was 17.37, but then Denis Kasputin jumped 17.24. In the third round Jonathan found the big one – 17.71 metres, the longest jump in the world in 2002. His fourth jump did not improve his position.

He passed in round five, when Garcia leapt into second place with 17.47 metres. In the final round Jonathan no-jumped, probably going for the really big one, but the gold was his. 'What a dog fight! I was just overwhelmed. I was on the point of crying on a number of occasions and had to choke back the tears. I couldn't believe what was happening: this awesome arena, the Olympic Games – and I was the champion!' In his lap of honour, Linford persuaded Jonathan to throw his shoes into the crowd, as Maurice Green had done.

As Jonathan reflected later on Sydney and its significance for him and his career, he said:

It was very important from the point of view of Alison. It would have been very hard for her had I lost. It would have come on top of what she was feeling in the loss of her mum. The mantra I had about Sydney was 'everything and nothing'. I had given everything, but actually it was nothing. If I had lost it would be hard to cope with, in the sense of feeling I had not achieved all that I could. Yet it is amazing how that one competition makes such a differ-ence. My career is viewed now in a completely different way, because of one competition.

I don't think I needed it as a person, although it is probably easier to say that having won. If I hadn't won, I am sure that I would always have looked back and said 'it would be nice to have won the Olympics'. I do smile when I think how differently I am viewed because I have won an Olympic gold medal – because really, what difference does it actually make? I suppose, in a sense, it was the human seal on my athletics career. But in reality it didn't make any difference – I am exactly the same person as if I had not won the Olympic gold. I am the world record holder, and the best triple-jumper there has ever been, but that wasn't influenced by Sydney.

Having been through Göteborg, and having seen the other side of the coin with not winning in Atlanta, and to a degree having always lived with a certain level of expectation and the unspoken disappointment that I never really lived up to 1995, it has made me much more realistic. I have a much better insight into who my real friends are and who are hangers-on. Success is a very illusory and shallow thing.

As he entered 2003, Jonathan was at peace about the future and a fifth Olympic Games. He said, 'I'm ready to retire; equally, I'm ready to carry on as long as my body will perform, and that's a nice position to be in.' In fact, the decision was largely made for him in two events at the end of the season.

His last event before the 2003 World Championships was at Crystal Palace, and there, at full speed, he hit the edge of the runway and fell awkwardly. He made an amazing recovery, competed in the World Championships, but withdrew after two jumps.

So ended the career of a great athlete. He explained to the press in Paris the background to his decision, beginning with the Bible:

I would like to preface what I say with a verse from the Bible. Proverbs 16, verse 9, says: 'A man devises a plan in his heart but God directs his path.' I probably thought God had directed my path off the triple-jump track at Crystal Palace two weeks ago and that was the end of my career. As I lay in the pit, that was what was going through my mind.

I thought I had broken my ankle, ruptured my ligaments and tendons, and I could not have walked if I had wanted to. I pretty much thought that was it and here endeth my career. Then, over the next few days, something quite miraculous happened, in that my ankle was not badly hurt at all. I sit here now feeling that almost a miracle has taken place.

I should not be here. I come back to Proverbs 16, verse 9. I had planned to carry on to the Olympics, but God directed his path [for me], so I will jump here and that will be the end of my career.

I am in great shape, good enough to go on to the Olympics next year and jump well, but I had always said I would carry on until my legs would take me no further or I felt God was saying something else. People have asked whether it might be a sign to carry on. All I can say is that, as I thought on my circumstances in the last couple of weeks, I felt sure this was the right thing to do.

Jonathan Edwards has been an outstanding athlete, and no one can take away the fact that in 1995 he broke the world record, and in 2000 took Olympic gold. But perhaps his greatest accolade comes from *The Times* journalist Andrew Longmore, '. . . an athlete capable of making sexy the intricate discipline of the triple jump'.

Olympic record

1988 – failed to qualify for final
1992 – failed to qualify for final
1996 – silver medal
2000 – gold medal

This chapter has been based on two exclusive interviews with Jonathan, in early 1996 and January 2001.

9

'More Than Gold'

A particularly significant development over the last few years has been the increasing recognition of the potential of major sporting events as evangelistic opportunities. While the Church has traditionally been suspicious of sports events – at times almost deliberately arranging services so that they clashed with a World Cup final or the opening ceremony of the Olympic Games – they have now come to see such events as an opportunity for witness and service.

Two things have happened in recent years to change that. First, alongside the Olympics and the football World Cup, a range of other major sporting events has developed. There are now World Cups in rugby union and rugby league, cricket, track and field athletics (every two years), as well as a growing number of regional events – European Football Championships, European Track and Field Championships, the Pan American, All African, Asian Games etc. The list stretches to at least 30 such major sporting events. Some of these regional events may have more significance in their region than even the Olympics or football World Cup.

In referring only to major sports events, we are omitting annual British sports events such as Wimbledon, the British

Grand Prix, the Open Golf, the FA Cup Final, the London Marathon, the Grand National – all of which make a significant impact, not only on the immediate area in which they take place but, through television, on the country generally.

The second major development has been technological. Even before the digital revolution it was possible to have, in the UK, four dedicated sports channels on your television. This accessibility means that it is almost irrelevant in which country the major sports event is taking place since the action comes simultaneously into your living room. With so many television channels available, an event that may have been accorded an hour's highlights 20 years ago is now shown live for several hours each day.

The Christian ministry to major sporting events began on a very modest scale in 1968, at the Winter Olympics in Grenoble, with some ministry taking place. The first (unofficial) chaplains operated in 1972 in Munich, and found themselves in the middle of a crisis when terrorists held hostages and murdered some of the competitors.

However, big-event ministry as we would recognise it today effectively began in 1988, both at the Summer Olympics in Seoul, Korea, and at the Winter Olympics in Calgary, Canada. There was now an official Olympic chaplaincy and event-specific literature.

During the following 16 years big-event strategy has evolved, with the initial focus being on the competitors themselves, along with the spectators who came to watch the event live. Later on, the vision spread to encouraging churches to try to use the interest in the major event in their city as a bridge for ministry to present the gospel to the residents of an event's host city. Then, as the television revolution took hold, it became obvious that approaches aimed at reaching people in the Olympic or World Cup host country could equally be applied in any city or country in the world, when the event was given a significant television profile. A point that needs to be understood here is that even when a major sports event comes to a particular city, most residents are unable to obtain tickets – and so finish up watching the event, in their own city, on television.

When the International Bible Society developed an evangelistic booklet in the form of a souvenir programme for the 1988 Seoul Olympics, it was an experiment, but it proved to be one of the most significant developments in the history of sports ministry. Major event-specific literature, in the form of an attractive, cringe-free, souvenir booklet on the event, has now become a central focus of major-event ministry.

In contrast to the traditional dull, religious, cheap Christian tract, these booklets are high-quality, full-colour and attractive pieces of literature. They are aimed at the non-Christian sports fan, and at least half the content is straight sport with the gospel being introduced gradually and in the language of sport. An important feature of these booklets has been to include factual information of the type that the fan is looking for – for example, a schedule of events and kick-off times with spaces to write in the results. This encourages the recipient to keep the booklet throughout, and even beyond, the event.

Two quotations from an American publication called *Mobilizer* (Fall 1995) provide a useful commentary on the development of major-event ministry: 'For more than twenty years, believers interested in ministering to and with excellent sportspersons have met to share ideas, receive training and encourage one another. Out of this history have come models of major sport event-related outreaches, multi-language literature for distribution, the co-operation of radio and video ministries and many other helps for local church and agency leaders.' Also, 'The materials will be available to churches around the world. This is a major shift in Olympic type outreach. No longer do you have to think that the host city is the place to evangelise. Now any city in almost any country can use the mega-event to show the love of Christ.' The first quotation is unattributed, the second is from Bill Sunderland.

For the 2000 Olympics, the major Christian publishers created about 20 different Christian resources. These included literature, video, CD, websites, sports gospels and New Testaments (scripture portions with a sporty cover and including the faith stories of some relevant Christian sportspersons). While primarily created for the host country, many of these resources were translated into several languages for worldwide distribution.

To help us understand how the ministry has developed, let us look in turn at different categories of ministry.

Competitors

Major sports events have proved wonderful opportunities to put Christian literature and other resources into the hands of competitors from countries where it is difficult to obtain Christian material. It would be hard to estimate how many Olympic athletes, for example, have received a Jesus Film or Sports New Testament while competing in a major event.

At every Olympics there is an official chaplaincy within the Olympic Village where the competitors live. At one level there is an opportunity for athletes to attend a service and to take part in a communal act of worship. However, it goes much further than that, with chaplains seeking opportunities to befriend athletes and simply to spend time with them. Athletes, who may not feel a need for prayer 364 days of the year, often welcome prayer the night before their Olympic final.

A typical day for the chaplains might include a variety of things – a meeting with other chaplains for prayer, praise and reporting back, followed by a morning walk through the Village, making contact with athletes in coffee bars or snooker halls. Then keeping an appointment with a believer in need of encouragement, accompanying an individual or a group to training, perhaps taking an athlete shopping – practical ways of serving those far from home, in an unfamiliar environment. Often the chaplains are involved in arranging hospitality for athletes or their families, perhaps in local Christian homes, and they will eat meals with athletes, building friendships that may last beyond the event itself. Chaplains will pray through discouragement together, seeking new openings, and lead or attend evening service in the chapel.

Andrew Wingfield Digby was chief chaplain at Seoul in 1988, and stressed the service element in the work: 'It is often a case of just being there as a Christian minister, making oneself available to whoever needs help, encouragement, prayer or just company. There are opportunities to share one's faith, but in general it is not appropriate, at least, by the chaplains. The brief is: be available, but don't get in the way.'

Chaplains to the 1991 World Student Games in Sheffield had the amazing experience of a Chinese student who came late one night and said simply in his faltering English, 'Want to become Christian – you have application form?' One of the chaplains had the delight of explaining to him how to become a Christian.

There can be significant opportunities for witness by athletes who are themselves Christians, in the midst of competition. In 1988 Violet McBride was vice-captain of the Great Britain women's hockey team, which finished fourth, just missing a medal. The very simple act of doing a daily Bible reading was noticed by her team-mates. Some of the girls would ask her, 'What is the word for today?'

Violet McBride was glad of the presence of the chaplains in Seoul: 'In the midst of all the activity and pressure, I appreciated the chaplains. When I arrived, there was a note from one of the chaplains waiting for me, saying that they were around. I went to the chapel services as often as I could. Two team-mates – neither of them Christians as far as I know – often came with me. One of them was injured before the competition. The chaplains prayed for her and she recovered and was able to play in the last match.'

Spectators

When the Olympic Games was held in Atlanta in 1996, the local Christian community saw it as a great opportunity for presenting the gospel to visitors to their city. Quest '96 produced a leaflet called 'When the world looks to Atlanta, will it see Christ in our community?' Inside, the theme was developed: 'Will they see Stone Mountain, Underground Atlanta, our beautiful tall buildings and the Braves? Will they focus on crime, racial tensions and political differences? Or will they see the followers of Christ working together to strengthen our community and to show compassion and love to a needy generation?'

Huge outreach initiatives, such as handing out cold water at venues, running concerts and radio shows and hosting athletes' families, were all part of the Christian presence in the city during the Games. In addition to this, there was a specific witness to the athletes, although this was on a much smaller scale.

The Christian people of Atlanta really took the opportunity to serve with both hands. There were hospitality suites on five sites to serve the visiting spectators; and the Southern Baptist Church had booths in the official visitor centres, and gave out visitor packs, containing peanuts, a map, some Christian literature, etc. Atlanta International Ministries provided a free babysitting service for hotels as a form of witness. An ambitious project called 'Atlanta Host' provided 3000 bed-and-breakfast places in Christian families for visitors, competitors' friends and families. All were given Bibles in their own languages.

Five evangelistic rallies were held in the city with Olympic athletes sharing their testimony each time. YWAM had 5000 kids working in Atlanta, of whom 1000 worked as security volunteers in the Olympic Village, in order to be involved as Christians. Other YWAM people did sports coaching and clinics with local churches.

The Salvation Army co-ordinated a venture involving churches offering six million cups of cold water on the streets to passers-by. The starting point for this highly successful venture was the fact that cold drinks are often a rip-off in tourist spots. By offering cold water free, the local Christians were not only being scriptural ('. . . a cup of water in the Lord's name . . .', see Matthew 10:42) and demonstrating Christian love, but also on occasions creating opportunities to share something of the faith that motivated them. Inevitably, perhaps, some of the churches offered the water in cups with the words of a Bible verse – for example, John 3:16 – printed on them!

The two main pieces of literature at this event were the souvenir booklet produced by the International Bible Society, *More Than Gold*, and the Interactive Guide to the Games, produced for the Southern Baptist Church. Five million copies of the latter were distributed in about six languages.

The Games generated a great number of souvenir pin badges, and a very innovative evangelistic approach was the production of a 'More Than Gold' badge, a phrase based on 1 Peter 1:7, '. . . your faith, of greater worth than gold . . .' Some 11 million badges were distributed, many at the Games with, typically, a local Christian presenting it, saying, 'May I give you a badge? Let me explain what it means.'

What could be more important than a gold medal for your country during the Olympics? The Christians of Atlanta were keen to tell as many of their guests as possible the answer to that question. Before the Games, it was the prayer of Christians in Atlanta that visitors to the Games would also encounter Jesus in the actions and words of the local Christians. They worked hard to ensure that their prayer was abundantly answered.

The world

With the explosion in sport on television, the opportunities for worldwide ministry at sports events have also exploded. As the report on the 2000 Olympics below shows, the development of high-quality international resources and training in ministry strategies has led to a massive increase in major sports-event ministry worldwide.

Olympics 2000

The Sydney 2000 Olympic and Paralympic Games will be remembered for many years as the 'Best Games Ever'. This comment, made by Juan Antonio Samaranch at the conclusion of these Olympics, reflected the culmination of seven years of intense planning and preparation by the Sydney Organising Committee for the Olympic Games, the City of Sydney and various other organising bodies.

The Sydney Games will also go down on record as the largest Christian community outreach in the history of the Sydney churches. Approximately 45 denominations and para-church ministry groups participated, along with 700 churches, to stage the outreach, not just in Sydney but across Australia. There are many reasons for the success of the Christian outreach in Sydney and Australia, the main one being that planning began early. Like the official SOCOG organising body, many of the key individuals who steered the planning and implementation of the Christian programmes began the development of the outreach in 1993, a full seven years before the outreach was staged.

'Quest Australia – More Than Gold' facilitated the largest Christian community outreach on record during the Sydney 2000 Olympic and Paralympic Games. The following statistics reflect the size and magnitude of the outreach that was implemented, leading up to and during the Games:

- 700-plus athletes' family members were hosted in Christian homes as part of the Samsung Athletes' Family Host 2000 programme.
- 110 sports outreaches were held by 85 churches, with 2500 youths attending. Some 1200 youths wanted to know more about Jesus, including 500 who made first-time commitments.
- 700-plus volunteers signed up through Quest to serve as

official chaplains, drivers, interpreters and administrative staff within SOCOG.

- Approximately 3000 Mission Team members assisted the local churches in outreach and service to the masses during the Games. Many of them utilised pin-trading, balloon sculpting, clowning, costumes, and even fire eating, to open a conversation with people.
- Approximately 224,000 people attended 120 Torch Run and Opening Ceremony festivals, staged by 500 churches across Australia.
- 3500 people had a cruise on the *Church on the Water* ferry. This was a creative venture by one church, which took people on a boat trip round the harbour free of charge and invited them to a service on board!
- The Salvation Army co-ordinated the distribution of 250,000 cups of water, tea and coffee, inside and outside of Olympic venues during the Games.
- 2500 creative arts performers sang, danced and acted at 155 venues during the Games, and 4500 hours of entertainment were staged for the purpose of drawing a crowd to hear the gospel.
- Over one million sports resources were distributed in the period leading up to and during the Games, with a variety of different Christian resources being produced for the Games. Six years before, no Christian sports resource had existed in Australia.
- Over 700 churches participated in the 'More Than Gold' outreach across the country.
- It was conservatively estimated that 2250 commitments of faith were made during the Games.
- The Bible Society in Australia sold more copies of its Sports New Testament than any other New Testament on record (225,000).
- The 'More Than Gold' stage show, produced by Logosdor, was seen by estimated audiences of 200,000 people around the world.

- 300 radio stations on five continents received Christian coverage of the Games via 2K Plus International Sports Media.
- Approximately 100,000 Australian dollars-worth of pin badges was sold by the Quest office leading up to and during the Games – that represents 10,000 pins. (If you have never been to the Olympics you would not believe the interest in collecting and trading the special Olympic pin badges which are produced by National Olympic Committees, sponsors, etc. There are even areas of the city designated specially for pin-trading.)
- It is estimated that over one million people walked past the 'More Than Gold' tent located at one of the main entrances to Olympic Park. This tent represents the first time ever that a religious organisation has been officially sanctioned to distribute materials in an Olympic venue. Some 300-plus people per hour visited the facility, and approximately 200,000 resources were distributed from this location to visitors, volunteers, officials and athletes.

As mentioned already, the success of the Quest Australia and 'More Than Gold' campaigns can be traced back several years. As soon as the announcement of the award of the Games to Sydney was made, Christian leaders began to cast the vision of major sports event outreach to denominational and para-church ministry leaders.

In 1996 a group of them visited the Olympic Games in Atlanta, to witness first-hand what ministry at a major event looked and felt like, experiencing the successes and failures of the ministry taking place there.

They began to raise financial support/'seed' money to hire a CEO and implement a front office, and in 1997 a CEO was employed to oversee the day-to-day operation of the organisation. Quest defined its strategy as follows:

Vision: The Christian community serving and sharing through the Olympic and Paralympic experience.

Mission: To capitalise on the opportunities provided by the 2000 Games to reach and teach people about Jesus Christ.

Strategic objectives: To cast the Vision of how the 2000 Olympics and Paralympics could be used for ministry:

- To energise and empower the Christian community for service and outreach.
- To facilitate and co-ordinate the development of Christian ministries leading up to and throughout the 2000 Games.
- To support and serve the athletes and the Olympic/ Paralympic communities.
- To encourage national and international partnerships between Christian organisations with a heart for mission and ministry.

Quest's structure included teams responsible for sports ministry, festivals, creative arts, athletes' family hosting, prayer, resources, children, communications, chaplaincy, evangelism, etc. Big-event ministry is still in its infancy, and at each event lessons are learned which are then applied in the next event in the cycle. The chief executive of Quest Australia is now assisting the churches in Greece to develop a programme of ministry for 2004.

Spreading around the globe

The type of ministry is very flexible, according to the local situation and the aims of the local organisers. It cannot be denied that major sports-event ministry is an excellent way of drawing people into a Christian community for the first time, and of helping them to find faith in Christ.

The Quest Australia catalogue listed over 30 different 'More Than Gold' resources and merchandise which were available to the Christian community around the period of the Sydney Olympics (September/October 2000). However, as far as the worldwide 'More Than Gold' ministry was concerned, there were six main evangelistic resources:

- 'More Than Gold' Interactive Guide
- 'More Than Gold' CD
- 'More Than Gold' Jesus Film
- 'More Than Gold' *Sports Spectrum* magazine
- *Beyond the Gold* video
- *The Prize* devotional booklet

The 'More Than Gold' ministry had the following impact:

- A major 'More Than Gold' ministry campaign occurred in about 25 countries and there was 'More Than Gold' activity of some kind in about 100 countries.
- The 'More Than Gold' Interactive Guide was a 32-page booklet produced by IBS/Dime. The contents were roughly: history 6 pages, results 16 pages, quotations/features 6 pages, gospel 4 pages. It contained a tear-off reply card to enable the reader to obtain more information about the Christian faith (in some versions, it was just a coupon within the booklet). A total of 939,000 copies of the booklet was distributed in 10 languages in about 100 countries (including a significant number of cases where English booklets were used in a country where English is not the main language).
- A computer CD containing music, sports action and testimonies of Olympians was used in 60 countries.
- The Jesus Film Project produced a special edition of the Jesus Film, with a 15-minute introduction of sports action and testimony. Over a million copies were distributed around the world in 43 languages.
- Three different versions of a special edition of *Sports Spectrum* magazine were produced for the USA, Australia and the Middle East.
- A Christian video called *Beyond The Gold* was distributed in

over 70 countries – at least 25,000 copies – and broadcast on at least 17 television networks. It was offered in eight languages – Arabic, English, French, Mandarin, Mongolian, Polish, Russian and Spanish.

- Scripture Union published *The Prize*, a 64-page booklet consisting of 20 athletes' testimonies, each with a Bible passage and a devotional comment. The booklet was translated into 12 languages and well over 100,000 copies were distributed in about 30 countries.
- Some highlights of the worldwide ministry included the production of the first-ever piece of Christian sports literature in Albanian – the Interactive Guide. The entire Polish Olympic delegation received a copy of the 'More Than Gold' Jesus Film before setting out for Sydney.
- 5000 copies of the Romanian language Interactive Guide were distributed in Moldova, mainly through Christians involved at a high level in Tae-Kwondo in the country. A further 10,000 copies were distributed by churches, in the parks of Bucharest, at metro stations, in universities, in orphanages, in a sports school and in the streets.
- Ministry in about 150–200 countries is anticipated by the 2004 Olympics.

10

Penny Heyns, Record-breaking Swimmer

Penny Heyns was born in Gauteng, South Africa, in November 1974. Growing up by the coast, she learned to swim at an early age. At about 12 she joined a swimming club and by the time she was 13 she was already swimming at representative level for the Natal Primary Schools.

In 1987 she came third in the 100m breaststroke in the South African Schools Championship, repeated the feat the following year and then, in 1989, came first. For the next three years she was the South African Schools champion in the 100m and 200m breaststroke.

At that stage, she was already plotting the future: 'I always set goals that were challenging but attainable, and I realised when I was about 14 that I had some potential and that I might become the South African champion. As South Africa was not allowed to compete internationally, I never really thought further than competing nationally.'

In her early high school years, there was no heated swimming pool where she lived, so Penny did a lot less training than swimmers would do today. There was fitness training on the beach, but not so much swimming. In any case, swimming didn't have all her attention; she also played representative hockey and made the District Track and Field team.

Another significant foundation in her life had already been set at this stage – her Christian faith:

> I was raised in a Christian home and always went to Sunday School and church. When I was about eight years old, we had visiting preachers at the church who stayed over at our house. They must have said something that challenged me, because I remember waking up and feeling that I needed to invite Jesus into my life. I did that and there was no turning back. Of course there are ups and downs and life can be a roller-coaster, but when you give your life to the Lord, the Holy Spirit always keeps you conscious of that, and even when you stray he always calls you back.
>
> Over the years I have come to realise that being a Christian is so much more than just going to church, reading the Bible and saying a quick prayer before carrying on living your life as you please. It means having an intimate relationship with Jesus and letting him be in complete control of your life. Living intimately with the Lord has been an exciting journey that has brought more joy and fulfilment than any other achievements I've ever been blessed with. The most exciting moment is yet to come when I meet my Lord face-to-face. The journey is not over yet and I believe it never will be.

By 1989 Penny was also competitive in the National Championships, taking third place in the 200m. In 1991 she was South African Champion in both the 100m and 200m. Her dream, you would think, would have been to swim in the Olympics – but it wasn't! South Africa had been banned from Olympic competition in 1960 because of the apartheid policy. 'Growing up, I didn't know anything about the Olympics,' she explains. Then the ban was lifted for the 1992 Olympics, and a 17-year-old Penny was chosen as the youngest competitor in the South African team for Barcelona.

Going to the Olympics should have been a dream, but it turned into a nightmare. First of all, there was an issue over her selection:

In the trials there were no specific criteria for selection, and that led to controversy. I did not win either of my races, but I had the fastest times in the trials. In the 100 metres I did a fast time in the heat, but was beaten in the final in a slower time. In the 200 metres I did not make the final, but won the B final in a faster time than the winner of the A final. I was selected on the basis of my times, but some people were up in arms, saying that it was unfair on the girls who had won the trials races.

The whole time I was preparing for Barcelona, all this was going on around me. Some of the press were saying it wasn't certain that I would be going and so on. It was hard to concentrate on my preparation and training. So when I finally got to Barcelona, rather than it being the highlight of my life so far, I was thinking 'Let's just get this over and done with', because by that stage it had become a nightmare.

As it was so long since South Africa had competed internationally, the team's preparation was not as good as it should have been. Penny was unsure what to expect at the Olympics and felt 'overwhelmed and intimidated' by it all. She did not do herself justice, finishing thirty-third in the 100m and thirty-fourth in the 200m. It was almost the end of a swimming career before it began. 'After the 1992 Olympics, I was so shocked and disillusioned with my performance that I thought it was time to retire.'

The decision was complicated by the fact that she had been

offered a swimming scholarship to the University of Nebraska, in the USA. She recalls a time of turmoil:

> Much of my time in Barcelona after my races was spent soul-searching and trying to work out what to do next – to take the swimming scholarship and go to Nebraska, or to stay in South Africa and effectively give up swimming. In myself I didn't want to swim any longer and I didn't want to go to America. But, as a Christian, I prayed about it rather than make the decision myself. And as I prayed about it I felt the Lord wanted me to go to Nebraska. So I went.

To understand Penny's strength of feeling about not going to America, you have to realise that she was 'a kid who loved being at home and who didn't even sleep over at other people's homes'. But in her heart she knew God wanted her to go to Nebraska so, despite her own preferences and feelings, she went. It was typical of Penny's attitude to her swimming:

> I believe there is a reason and a purpose for everything, and if God creates us with a package of talents or gifts, there is a reason for that. I just feel that it was my responsibility to develop those talents to the best of my ability. I never wanted to retire and look back and wonder if I had done everything I could with what God had given me. From an early age the Lord was part of my swimming all the way. Even when I did not have a desire to swim, I was obedient to what I thought he was calling me to do.
>
> Swimming has in some ways been my 'classroom' where God teaches me so much about his ability and [to have] faith in him. I love the sense of satisfaction that I get when I've done a swimming workout or race, and know that I gave my whole being and heart to God in every moment of the swim. It's the best worship I can offer him.

The time in Nebraska could have started better:

> The journey to Nebraska was via Europe and it took two days, so that was quite scary in itself. Then, when I arrived, they had forgotten that I was coming, so I sat at the airport for an additional four hours – until they remembered to collect me.
>
> Then, when I went to my room on campus, the girl in the room was not expecting to have to share with anyone. Fortunately, she was a Christian too, so we got on OK. Settling down in Nebraska wasn't easy, but the Lord provided for me. It was quite a testing time but I grew a lot spiritually, and every time I had a problem God seemed to bring Christian people across my path.

The swimming was a shock to the system too. In South Africa Penny was used to swimming a maximum of four kilometres a session, usually once a day – albeit very high-intensity work. She wasn't used to the distances they swam at Nebraska, and it took her almost a whole season to adjust to the training, refocus her goals, and take charge of where she wanted to go with her swimming.

At Nebraska she regained the desire to swim again. Working with her coach, Jan Bidrman, she realised that by changing a couple of things in her stroke, she could improve. Her times began to get faster. The fact that she was not used to the intensity of the training in Nebraska had a positive side too: she arrived reasonably fresh and still had a lot of potential to develop.

From 1993 to 1996 Penny was based at the University of Nebraska, which she represented in the NCAA (University Championships). She picked up a first place, three second places, and a third place in those championships.

In 1994 she took part in two international competitions: the Commonwealth Games and the World Championships. In the Commonwealth Games, she took bronze in the 100m and came sixth in the 200m. In the World Championships she reached the final of the 100m, coming sixth. That race was won by Samantha Riley in a new world record time, something that was to have a big effect on Penny:

> After my first year in Nebraska I had changed my stroke and adjusted my goal. The goal for that season was to get to the Commonwealth Games, which I did, and got a bronze medal. Then I went to the World Championships in Rome, and was swimming in the race in which Sam Riley broke the world record. Being involved at that level and seeing her stroke, I realised that breaking the world record was an attainable goal.

The year 1995 was another one of progress for Penny. She won the 100m and 200m in the World Student Games and the All Africa Games. In the Pan Pacific Games she picked up a first and second and, as far as times were concerned, she was about one second outside the world record. By then she was realising that if she continued to improve, by the following year she too could break the world record – and that is what happened.

It was in March 1996 in the South African Olympic trials in Durban that Penny broke the world record for 100m, swimming a time of 1:07.46, and beating Samantha Riley's existing record by 0.23 seconds.

She entered the 1996 Olympics as world number one and quickly stamped her authority on the event, breaking her own world record in a heat, in a time of 1:07.02. The final was a tough race. Penny led from the start, but came under great pressure from a 14-year-old American girl, Amanda Beard. Amanda was catching Penny on the final length, but Penny just hung on to become the first South African Olympic champion for 44 years. The time was 1:07.73, with Beard 0.36 slower, and Samantha Riley in third place.

The 200m followed a similar pattern. Penny set a new record – an Olympic record – in the heats. In the final she established a solid lead early in the race, but Amanda Beard closed the gap all the way home. Penny set a new Olympic record in 2:25.41 to win by 0.34 seconds. This time Agnes Kovacs of Hungary took bronze, ahead of Samantha Riley. Penny had become the first swimmer ever to take both breaststroke events in the same Olympics, and she narrowly missed a medal in the 4×100m medley relay, where South Africa came fourth.

She reflected on the achievement later:

The two races were very different. Since I was already the 100 metres world record holder, I was the favourite and was expecting to win and break the world record. In the heat in the morning I had a great swim and was disappointed with the time of 1:07.02 – even though it was a new world record. I had expected to be under 1:07. I thought several swimmers would be close to my existing world record.

I hoped to break the world record again in the final, and every time I swam I was hoping to improve. I figured that in the evening I could do it. But what I didn't take into account was that if you break a world record in the morning, the media spend time with you. It was only the second time in my life that I had broken a world record, and I got excited by it all, and it was hard to settle down and think about doing it again in the evening. Also, as it was the Olympic final, the focus was more on winning the race than on the time. As I analysed my performance in the final afterwards, perhaps I had tried too hard and had taken a few more strokes than I needed to. I still won the race, but perhaps it cost me the record.

The 200 was a bit of a surprise! At that stage I felt I was a much better 100 metres swimmer. But I realised that if I swam my best, I would have a chance of winning. My approach was to go out as fast as I could and hope to get a big enough lead that no one could catch me. It worked

– just! The last 50 metres of the 200 final were so hard that I think the Lord carried me all the way to the finish.

It was wonderful to be a double Olympic champion – the just reward for all those hours of effort in training. However, Penny still kept it all in perspective:

When you win an Olympic gold medal, people think you should feel on top of the world. But I realised that I was a Christian and that, even though I had swum with all my heart to glorify the Lord, there were areas where I wasn't being obedient, and I wasn't giving 100 per cent. I knew that if I wasn't living as God wanted me to, a gold medal in itself would not bring fulfilment in life.

Even though I was a Christian, I knew I was looking for my identity through my sport. Suddenly I had achieved what every athlete aspires to, and I still wasn't fulfilled. The Olympics changed my life. I recommitted my life to Jesus and started taking my relationship with him seriously. That decision impacted everything.

In early 1998 Penny really wanted to retire from swimming:

I thought it was time for me to move on. I hated swimming. I had no desire to swim, no respect for the sport.

As I look back now at the years after 1996, the danger for athletes is that it becomes so important for you to improve and to achieve the goal – whatever it is – and if you are not doing it for the right reason, you walk away empty. I think in 1996 I had achieved all that and got the adulation from people around and was left wondering 'What do I really think about it?' With success comes the pressure that you have got to do it again. If you don't have your priorities right, and you don't know why you are doing it – which should be to glorify God – then you can easily feel a bit low, confused and empty.

In 1998 I was still living in Nebraska, but my coach had moved to Calgary. As I prayed about it, I felt that God was telling me to go to Calgary. I went, much more in a spirit of obedience to him than thinking about swimming. I went because I felt in my gut that God wanted me to go to Calgary. I didn't think he necessarily wanted me there for swimming. I thought that perhaps he wanted to use me in Calgary in some other way.

I never thought I would ever again swim close to what I had done in 1996. But, as I put my mind to it and trained hard, I started to improve again. But it was different. This time I was swimming just because I felt God wanted me to, not because I really wanted to for myself.

Jan and Penny set a goal of swimming her fastest 100m race since Atlanta in the Goodwill Games, and this mission was accomplished as Penny won the 100m and the 200m as well as breaking a world record at 50m.

After the 1998 World Championships she decided not to take part in the South African Commonwealth Games trials. When people questioned her about it, she said that she was praying about it and waiting for the Lord to show her what to do:

A lot of people did not understand that. There was even a chance of losing my main sponsor over it. To me it was an easy decision – people can give sponsorship or withdraw it, but ultimately God is the provider.

My faith was in the Lord and I stuck to what I believed, and the fact that I didn't go to the Commonwealth Games – as the Federation would not choose me as I had not done the trials – didn't really bother me. Perhaps sitting out the end of that season was part of the reason why I broke the world record in 1999, because I was rested. Perhaps God really does know best!

The year 1999 was an amazing one. She took three second places at the World Short Course Championships, then from July to September 1999, she set 11 new world records. At the Janet Evans Invitational in California in July, Penny set new world records in the heats and final of the 100m and 200m breaststroke. The following month in Sydney, in the Pan Pacific Championship, she broke her own record in the 100m for five world records in five consecutive races. Just for good measure, she set two more world records in the 200m and also broke the world 50m record in a special time trial.

To break 11 world records in three months was unprecedented in the history of swimming. She held five of the six breaststroke world records simultaneously, again unprecedented. How on earth did she manage that?

You always have a chance to break records at major competitions, because you are well prepared and in peak condition. It also stands to reason that if the competition is late in the year and you have worked hard all through the season, you should be producing fast times.

But 1999 was a bit of a surprise when I set four world records – the 100 and 200 twice each – in two days in Los Angeles. It was in the middle of the season and I was in the middle of a period of my hardest training in gym work ever. I was so tired before the race that I just thought, 'I am going to swim up and down and praise the Lord and worship him through my talents', hoping that I could just produce a half decent time so that my coach would be satisfied. But God blew my mind with the world records!

There were a number of factors contributing to the records. I had stepped up my training to a different level. The preparation was more intense and focused. I was also getting the rest I needed. My diet was right. I trained with all my heart and there were no distractions. It was a culmination of all that, and the work I had put in during the previous seasons. Also, because there was no expectation, I was relaxed and able to enjoy it.

After such a phenomenal season in 1999, Penny was a clear favourite to retain her two Olympic titles, but it did not happen. She failed to reach the final of the 200m and only came third in the 100m.

Penny's own analysis of the whole situation is as follows:

After what I did in 1999 I had great expectations for 2000, and with it being the Olympic year, that added pressure. I so badly wanted to do the same again, but a number of things culminated in my being over-trained, and it just didn't really work out.

In the Olympics, things didn't go the way I expected them to. My first event was the 100 metres. The heat was in the morning and the semi-final in the evening. In the first race, I realised that something was wrong because my legs were so tired. Ten metres from the end I was dying. [She won the heat in 1:07.85.] In the semi-final I decided to start off a little slower and save some energy for the finish, but it didn't really work as I felt I was dying even sooner in that race. [She came third in 1:08.33.]

When I got to the final my coach and my supporters were panicking, not knowing what was happening. I just felt, 'All I can do is swim with all my heart from the start. If I am meant to achieve something, God will carry me to the finish. If not, whatever happens will be for the best.' So I just put my trust in him and went out and swam. I was satisfied that I did the best I could. [She came third in 1:07.55.]

On the day I did the best I could with where I was at. There is no explaining why I wasn't in the same form as I was in 1999. I had done everything the same, and harder. The only thing I can think of was the pressure and the effort of travelling back and forward to South Africa for appearances, those added things in an Olympic year.

My only regret is, perhaps, that I got my years mixed up. If I could have swum in Sydney the times I did in 1999, I would have come away with two gold medals.

That there was a different attitude to her swimming after 1998 is well illustrated in the following incident:

In 2000 it was more apparent that my heart was not in it. In February 2000 a team-mate of mine was in a car accident and subsequently died. I knew her well and, when the accident occurred, I spent a week at the hospital with her family, and I wondered if perhaps that was the reason why I was in Calgary. With hindsight – although I would not change it – I think spending that week in the hospital affected my preparation for Sydney. If I had had, in 2000, the mindset I had in 1996, I wouldn't have spent any time at the hospital. I would have gone to the World Short Course Championship, instead of cancelling it to spend time with the family.

There were other decisions that she made 'because of where I stood spiritually, that may have negatively affected my swimming. But I do believe that swimming isn't everything in life.'

Penny, too, sees a silver lining in the cloud of not retaining her titles:

In 1998 someone in Nebraska said to me, 'The next medal that you win will be the one that opens the hearts of your nation.' At the time I didn't understand it and I also thought, 'I swim two races [100m and 200m] and expect medals in both, so why is she talking about medal, not medals?' But when I got that bronze in Sydney, I had peace, and felt that was what she was talking about. This was part of God's plan.

Since then I have understood that, had I won, it would have been so difficult for me to speak to kids and say, 'You don't always win, but you have to learn to trust God and learn from those failures.' Because I did not win I had a better platform to speak from. Before that, people could have said, 'It is easy for you to talk about having faith in God as you always win!' So it was probably a greater testimony for me to come third and to deal with it in a godly way.

Early in 2001, at the age of only 26, Penny pulled down the curtain on her illustrious career. She said at a news conference:

I thought the way I was feeling may just have been a result of all the Olympic hype. So I didn't retire absolutely. But, having gone back to Canada, I don't think my heart is in it the way it was before. I used to say there was no way I would retire until I knew there was no way I could go any faster, but I was wrong. I really believe I could go faster, but I'm not prepared to make the sacrifices.

She elaborated on that later:

What I meant was that I really felt I could go faster but, for the previous eight years I had lived overseas, away from my family, and I had put everything into my training; and at that stage I didn't feel called to swim any longer. I still thought that with all my experience if I had another season, I would make good choices and could improve, but I really think that you always want to swim the perfect race and I don't think that ever comes. You are always hard on yourself and see something you could do better, which means you could swim faster.

Looking back, I know it was the right decision. If I had continued swimming I would have been in Calgary in May of 2001 when my mother passed away – very suddenly. If I had still been swimming I would not have spent the last two months of her life with her. I know that my swimming career ended when it should have done. I will always wonder if I could have swum faster if I had just kept going, but that isn't important any more.

In retirement, Penny Heyns is involved in public speaking and a property business, as well as doing some presenting on television.

Olympic record

1992
100m breaststroke – 33rd
200m breaststroke – 34th

1996
100m breaststroke – 1st, 1:07.73 (heat time 1:07.02 – world record)
200m breaststroke – 1st, 2:25.41 (Olympic record)
4×100m medley relay – 4th

2000
100m breaststroke – 3rd, 1:07.55
200m breaststroke – 20th, 2:30.17

Other career highlights

- The only woman in the history of the Olympics to win 100m and 200m breaststroke in the same Olympics
- First South African Olympic gold medallist for 44 years
- Broke a world record 14 times

- Set 11 world records in three months in 1999, unprecedented
- At one point she held five of the six women's breaststroke world records simultaneously

This chapter was written on the basis of an exclusive interview with Penny, September 2003.

11

Amanda Borden, Gymnastics Team Captain

Amanda Borden was born in Cincinnati, Ohio, on Tuesday 10 May 1977. Her family were Christians, so she was brought up in a Christian environment from day one and went to church regularly from childhood onwards. As she grew up she tried different sports, like soccer and T-ball, but at the age of seven everything changed.

Amanda was taking ballet lessons but a friend of her mother's commented that she looked more like a gymnast than a ballerina – probably because Amanda always 'looked real muscular'. And when Amanda heard that gymnastics included tumbling, she begged her mother to put her in a gymnastics class.

So she started gymnastics lessons – although at first it was only one hour a week. But almost immediately the coaches felt there was something special about her and moved her up to a higher level of training. This involved two hours a day, three days a week.

In 1984 the Olympics were held in Los Angeles, and Amanda watched some of the gymnastics on television. She was only seven years old so she didn't really understand what the Olympics were about, but she recalls loving Mary Lou Retton and, after the Olympics, her grandma went out and bought her a leotard that looked like the one Mary Lou wore in the Olympics. Perhaps that was the inspiration, but Amanda never really looked at Mary Lou and thought that would be *her* one day. It would be 12 years before the Summer Olympics returned to the USA. Amanda would be 19 then – but that comes later in the story.

Amanda then progressed to the Junior Elite testing, where they measure physical strength and flexibility, as well as basic gymnastics skills. She qualified for a one-week training camp in Tennessee, and by the age of 10 she was in the gym 12 hours a week. She began competing outside her own area and travelled around in the states of Ohio, Kentucky, Indiana and Michigan. Most importantly, she loved every minute of it. Her family travelled with her, and her brother, Bryan, would bring a friend along to keep him amused.

At this stage Amanda was not a dominant competitor. She would always do well on beam and floor, but never did well enough on bars to win the competition. But Amanda's mother recalls that, at a very early stage, judges were saying as they watched her on the floor that she would be special. In any case, for Amanda and her family, it was all about just having fun and doing the best she could.

The year 1990 proved to be another turning point. When Amanda turned 13 she moved her training to the Cincinnati Gymnastics Academy, and got a new coach, Mary Lee Tracy; and when she was about 13 she made the Level 10 national team, the so-called Junior Olympic team. Then her coach asked her if she wanted to try the next level up, which was Elite. At that stage she knew she was good at gymnastics, but didn't know if she could compete with the likes of Shannon Miller and all the big guys. However, she was willing to give it a try.

It has been said that the smartest career move Amanda made was to be born in Cincinnati where Mary Lee Tracy, an outstanding gymnastics coach, had her base. Ironically, before Amanda appeared on the scene, Mary Lee had no plans to coach to Elite level. However, she felt that with Amanda's talent it would be an injustice if she did not have the chance to go all the way. To some extent, Mary Lee and Amanda were on a journey together, learning from each other. They were a great partnership, and while Amanda would probably not have made it to the Olympics without Mary Lee's help, it is also the case that Mary Lee's reputation was enhanced by Amanda's success.

That Mary Lee was a Christian added a dimension to the relationship. They used to pray before every competition – not for victory, but for everyone to be safe and have fun in a great competition. Mary Lee also taught Amanda from an early age that she could only do her best, and that everything was ultimately in God's hands. Amanda is grateful as she looks back: 'Mary Lee helped me to know how to show others how to be a Christian. I began to see how my faith could tie into my life, not just as a person but also as a gymnast. She taught me that living for Christ is a daily thing rather than a church thing.'

At Cincinnati Gymnastics Academy, Mary Lee chooses a theme for each year, and the theme in Amanda's first year was, 'I can do everything through Christ who gives me strength' (Philippians 4:13). This almost became a career-long theme for Amanda: 'I liked those words. They told me I did not have control over what was going to happen so I needed to have faith in God that things would turn out all right.'

When she competed in the American Classic, at Tempe, Arizona, and managed a first, second and third, the evidence suggested that she was not out of her depth with the 'big guys'. In 1991 she came third for her age level at an Elite competition, and so qualified for her first US Championships. However, she broke her elbow and was in plaster for six weeks, then, on resuming training, she pulled a hamstring. The two injuries ended the year for her.

The year 1992 was an Olympic one, but Amanda had no serious expectations of making the US team. When she competed in the US National Championships, though, and was placed fifth, it gave her confidence as she headed for the Olympic trials. At the trials she finished seventh; her goal in the trials was not really to make the team – just to do the best she could – so when she finished seventh she shocked herself!

Because there are seven in an Olympic team, Amanda assumed that her seventh place would take her to the Olympics. Then, two weeks later, the team was announced: Amanda was out, and two gymnasts who had not competed in the Olympic trials because of injury were in. Amanda says:

Not making the team wasn't, at first, a shattered dream, as I had not really expected it anyway. I had done my best and performed to a high standard. That was all I could have done. As time passed it came to mean more to me.

What was disappointing was that I did qualify and they took it away. It was crushing to think that I was going to the Olympics, only to find out two weeks later that I wasn't going. I ended up almost quitting gymnastics over it.

As she thought about it, she decided not to let a decision by selectors, which was completely outside her control, determine her future. 'When I took a step back, I felt that I should listen to my own heart and not let anyone else tell me whether I wanted to be a gymnast or not. I decided that I still loved gymnastics and that I would continue despite the setback.'

The whole thing seemed very political, in that there seemed to be a feeling among the selectors that Amanda had come up through the ranks very quickly and was not as well known as the other gymnasts. It was said that she had too little international experience to be put into the biggest competition of all. Amanda's parents were told that one of the selectors had said that even if she had come first in the trials, they would not have taken her to Barcelona.

What made it even harder were the high expectations of the community, with the local television and newspaper constantly covering her. Then she was made alternate for the team and asked to be ready to go if anyone was injured.

The family tried to accept it and move on. As her mother put it, 'We truly believe that God has a plan, that the non-selection happened for a reason and that God knew what he was doing.' It is possible that had Amanda gone to the 1992 Olympics, she would not have carried on and 1996 would never have happened.

Amanda was rewarded for her decision to carry on, and 1993 was the year that really moved her up a stage. She began to travel and compete internationally: she finished fourth in the US National Championships and was chosen as alternate for the World Championships in England. She also competed in Nagano and Tokyo.

In 1993 Jaycie Phelps moved to Cincinnati Gymnastics, and together they rose to the top of the gymnastics world. They both qualified for the World Team Championships in 1994 in Germany, where the team won the silver medal. Amanda also went to Australia in 1994 for the World Championships, where she qualified for the uneven bar finals.

There was one small problem in Amanda's life as an international gymnast – they expected her to go to school as well! She says:

It was a busy schedule but it worked for me. When I was in high school I trained 6.00–8.30 a.m., then went off to school. After a full 9–3 school day, it was back to the gym until I was done, usually after four hours or more, finishing about 8 p.m. My teachers at Finneytown High School were really helpful and would give me work on Fridays so that I could prepare for the following week's work ahead of time. I had to give up my weekend but it meant that I wasn't as crunched on time the next week.

She certainly made an impact on the school and was chosen as 'Homecoming Queen', and was also a member of the National Honor Society and the Cum Laude Society.

Dropping Amanda off at the gym at 6 a.m. was the short straw for one of her parents, but Patty Borden is philosophical about it:

Most parents' lives are dominated by their kids' sport and activities. Ours was a bit more extreme, but not all that different. We were just trying to do what we could to make her dreams come true. We could never have dinner together during the week, but we tried to make Sunday a family day when we made up for the rest of the week, always trying to go to church and have dinner together.

The year 1995 was a mixed one for Amanda. It started well with two firsts and a third at the McDonald's American Cup in Seattle. In the Pan Am Games in Argentina she was elected team captain as the USA won the team prize, and Amanda had an individual first and two second places. The second half of 1995 didn't really happen, as a broken toe kept her out of competition. However, she had done enough to receive the US Gymnastic Sportswoman of the Year award.

The Olympic year of 1996 started well, and at the Budget Gymnastics Invitational in Miami Amanda scored really well, with a 9.725 on the bars, 9.775 on the beam, and 9.512 on the floor as her team took first place. Perhaps because of the 1992 experience or just because of her higher expectations, Amanda found the 1996 Olympic trials very demanding. She recalls:

The nerves were incredible. I had trained for 12–13 years to get to that point, yet it was all about how I performed on that one day. In a way there was more pressure here than at the actual Olympics.

I knew I wasn't the best gymnast in the trials and that I was competing for one of the lower places on the team. The competition was very tough but I took confidence from the fact that I knew I had prepared as well as I could. I believed, too, that whatever happened, God was in control and I was ready to accept whatever the outcome was.

When she came fifth in the trials, her place in the 1996 Olympic Games in Atlanta was secure. She was ecstatic to be on the team and 'honoured to be with girls I very much admired as both people and athletes'. But Amanda wasn't the only ecstatic Borden – she recalls looking up to the stands and seeing her mom and dad and brother, clapping and cheering and jumping around! Amanda's mother admits to being a nervous wreck during the trials, dreading that Amanda would finish up as the alternate again. When Amanda finished her routines and got good marks, Patty Borden was so thrilled and proud.

That the Games were in her own country was special for Amanda:

A lot of people have asked me if I would rather have done the Olympics in another country. Definitely not! It was so great to have the whole family come down and be there. My family has always been a huge part of my success and having them there was special. Having them share the Olympic experience and go to the Olympic village and see Centennial Park helped them celebrate all the hard work they had put into my career. Also, to be in our comfort zone, having our normal daily routine, being able to eat our typical food, played a big part in our success.

Then she was chosen as captain of the US Women's Gymnastics team:

Being chosen as captain by my team-mates was one of the biggest honours at the Olympics. I knew I could contribute with my routines, but I also knew that I wasn't the best athlete on the team. I felt that I could contribute by being a team leader and helping anybody out when they needed it. As team captain my job was basically to mediate between athletes, or between athletes and coaches. And just to communicate and make sure that everything was where it needed to be.

This was the Olympics and you want every athlete on the team to feel prepared, to feel ready, confident and comfortable. My job was very easy. Everyone got along really well. There were very few problems. I just pumped everybody up and gave pep talks when I needed to.

Team-mate Kerri Strug summed up why they chose her: 'Everybody likes Amanda. There's just something about her.' Luan Peszek, the editor of *US Gymnastics* magazine, added, 'She has such a great personality. [She] is a real showman, like a Mary Lou Retton. That smile of hers really captures the audience and the judges.'

Being captain was a role in which her faith in God became visible:

There was one of my team-mates who was very nervous. On the first day of the competition, I just sat down beside her and gave her a little pep talk. I said, 'We have all worked so hard for this and we have prepared mentally and physically. We are all healthy and strong and ready to go. Now it's in God's hands. You go out there and do your best and the rest is up to him. If our team is on fire tonight, and we win, that was his plan. If not, then we go out and give our best and we know that he had a different plan.'

Turning it over to God took away a lot of the stress and a lot of pressure off our backs. I felt we had done everything in our power, everything we had control over, and the rest was up to him.

OK, so she had made it to the Olympics – but that was just the beginning! As we said near the beginning of the book, for Baron de Coubertin, the founder of the modern Olympics, 'The important thing in the Olympic Games is not winning but taking part.' But the US team wanted to be more than just a part of the event. However, they were not favourites: a typical performance would be to finish second or third behind Romania or Russia.

The first decision for the US team concerned the opening ceremony. They would have loved to have been part of it, but the problem was that the opening ceremony was only two days before the gymnastics competition: 'We could have gone, but as we would have been on our feet for four hours, we opted not to. It was the same with the closing ceremony. It would have been fun to be there but, because of security and all that was going on, we opted to just watch it on television.'

As far as the competition was concerned, Amanda tried to treat it as much like any other competition as possible: 'I had trained so hard and I just went out to do my best for myself and the team. I compete better when I don't put too much pressure on myself. I couldn't have asked anything more. I competed on beam and floor – both compulsory and optionals. I made a few mistakes, but overall I did everything just about as good as I could.'

The result surpassed their expectations when the team took gold. Amanda was blown away!

Winning gold was incredible. When we walked out for the medal ceremony and heard 'USA, USA' being chanted, I just couldn't believe it. All of my dreams had come true. But hearing the national anthem being played for our team will always be etched on my heart. I remember going back to my room afterwards and my room-mate's, and my gold medals were sitting on the desk at the end of our bed. We kept saying to each other. 'Did we really do that? Did we really win gold?'

Having her family present, her long-term training partner Jaycie, and Mary Lee, one of the coaches to the Olympic team, really was the icing on the cake. On the final night the Bordens and other parents were in a box in the arena. Amanda's mother says that her daughter always had an uncanny knack of locating them even in the biggest arena – she could see them in the box!

In the immediate aftermath of the victory, the team was mobbed, and even took to wearing disguises when they went out in Atlanta! When Amanda and Jaycie returned home there were 2000 people at Fountain Square to meet them, a party in a school, and a parade. Finneytown and Cincinnati were so proud of their Olympic victors.

After the Olympics it was a manic time, when the Magnificent Seven were pictured on Wheaties boxes, posed on a balance beam for *Sports Illustrated*, met the First Family and toured the White House. They threw out the first pitch at a Cincinnati Reds game, were invited to appear on the soap opera *Days of Our Lives*, and were featured stars of a downtown rally honouring Cincinnati's Olympic athletes. They did *Today*, the *Letterman Show* and seemingly endless chat shows. They were treated as heroes wherever they went, and when they went on their tour they were like little rock stars, with fans screaming everywhere they went.

Going to the White House and meeting President Clinton was 'pretty cool for all of us'. The President had been in the arena when they won the gold, and seemed to know their names and all about them. They met all the other American Olympic athletes and all of them went to the White House together in one big plane, which was pretty exciting. The tiny gymnasts particularly enjoyed meeting basketball's dream team of seven-footers – simply the long and the short of Olympic success!

The Cincinnati Gymnastics Academy, where Amanda and team-mate Jaycie Phelps trained, didn't know what had hit them. As Lynne Ruhl said, 'We've never had to deal with this much attention before. I've lost count of the number of calls we received about the gymnasts. And I am only dealing with a portion of the calls. There are many avenues people are going through, and I'm only one of them. I get a ton [of requests] every day.'

At first the appearances were fun, and it was a relief to be together with the team and not to be under pressure. Looking back, Amanda feels she may have agreed to too many things, and exhausted herself criss-crossing the country to make appearance after appearance. But it was a unique experience and easier to evaluate in retrospect:

When I think back on my career now, after seven years out, I have a completely different perspective. Going through the tough times, I never really understood why they were happening. I would ask God, 'Why am I injured? Why am I not in this competition? Why me? I work so hard.'

I did have faith and I did believe he had a plan for me. But when you are stuck in it, you don't always see the plan. Without having faith in him and without trusting that he had that plan, I would never have made it through my gymnastics career. I had a lot of highs and a lot of lows, and he definitely sustained me in the lows. Looking back now, I can see that going through those lows was all about keeping my faith in him.

When I started, I didn't know that I would make the Olympic team, I didn't know that I would get an Olympic medal, but I did know that my career would be very successful and very worthwhile because God was part of it.

Amanda has made a permanent mark on her sport, and there is

now a move called the Borden BB – a straddle jump with a half jump on the balance beam. As Amanda explains, 'If you complete a skill in an international competition before anyone else, they will name it after you.'

Amanda had been so focused on the Olympics and doing her best that she had never really thought beyond that point. When it came she was suddenly unprepared as she had simply planned to go to college, like any normal person. After the Olympics, however, she found that a gold medallist is not a normal person, so she decided to turn professional and go on tour. She quickly got herself an agent. Gymnastics was originally her hobby, done after school, but now – suddenly – it was her job.

The next period of her life was spent in exhibitions, appearances, etc., exploiting the Olympic achievement. Soon, though, she was ready to become that 'normal' person. She studied at Arizona State as an Education major, and at the time of writing is about to start student teaching in Arizona.

Her days of competition are over; however, there are no regrets:

> I loved my time as a competitive gymnast, but I knew when it was time to move on. Getting my degree and becoming a teacher became my priority, so gymnastics has had to be put on the back burner and is pretty much out of my life as far as physically doing it is concerned. I still do gymnastics camps and some coaching and get a thrill from being able to help and inspire young people.

Most recently, Amanda has started an after-school programme for beginner gymnasts; so with her knowledge of gymnastics and the love she has for her sport, a new successful avenue seems imminent for Amanda.

Olympic record

1996
Gold

This chapter was written on the basis of an exclusive interview with Amanda, September 2003, and supplemented by e-mails and conversations with Amanda's mother, Mrs Patty Borden.

12

Olympic Trivia

Accident-prone or what?

Anne Ottenbrite of Canada won the 200m breaststroke in the Los Angeles Olympics in 1984, despite doing her best not to be there! Shortly before the Canadian trials she managed to dislocate her right kneecap while showing off a pair of shoes!

While in Los Angeles she was involved in a car crash and also managed to sustain a thigh strain while playing a computer game. Imagine if she had been injury-free!

The original naked chef

The first recorded Olympic champion was Coroebus of Elis, who won the 200m race – the only event in the year 776. The length of the race was based on a legend that Hercules had run this distance in one breath. Not a lot of people know this, but Coroebus was a cook – and competitors in those days, of course, competed nude.

Keeping up the tradition

When a *Sports Illustrated* reporter asked American goalkeeper Briana Scurry what she would do if the USA won gold in the 1996 Olympics, she replied that she would run naked through the streets of Athens, Georgia, where the final was played. Well, the USA won, so at 2 a.m. the next morning an honour-bound Scurry, accompanied by a friend with a video camera, did a 10-metre dash wearing only her gold medal!

Tarzan

Four Olympic medallists later played Tarzan in films:

1   Johnny Weismuller, who won two swimming gold medals, in 1924 and in 1928.
2   Buster Crabbe, who won a swimming bronze in 1928.
3   Hermann Brix, who won silver in the shot put in 1928.
4   Glen Morris, who took gold in the decathlon in 1936.

Other film careers

Harold Toshiyuki Sakata, silver medallist in 1948 in weightlifting, later appeared as a villain (Odd Job) in the James Bond film *Goldfinger*.

Another Olympic winner (with gold medal performances in equestrian events in 1968 and 1972) went on to appear in the films *Dead Cert* and *International Velvet*. The name? Cornishman V – a horse!

Running feat

In 1924, Finnish runner Paavo Nurmi won five gold medals, including the 1500m and 5000m in the space of just one hour.

Volunteers

About 50,000 volunteers are involved in staging the Olympic Games.

Tricky team-mate

In the 1912 marathon, Kennedy McArthur and Charles Gitsan, South African team-mates, were well ahead of the field. On the understanding that McArthur would wait for him, Gitsan stopped for a drink of water. McArthur then ran on and won by a minute and two seconds.

Nike

In 1992 Nike built an ambitious advertising campaign around the Olympics that somewhat backfired. The poster campaign focused on four of their sponsored competitors, and posters appeared around the world telling the public how successful their champions would be. A Michael Johnson poster congratulated the reader on doing '. . . something few athletes would ever do – passing Michael Johnson'. Unfortunately, a viral complaint resulted in no fewer than four people passing Michael, as he failed to reach the final.

Another poster, featuring the 1500m favourite Nourredine Morceli, asked, 'Ever heard the Algerian national anthem? You will.' Morcelli finished seventh.

Sergei Bubka was the hot favourite for the pole-vault. 'Spanish air traffic control has been notified' ran the poster. Bubka also failed to find his form and was out. The only one of Nike's four to succeed was Michael Jordan in the US basketball team.

Discontinued

The following were Olympic sports in the years listed, but are no more:

Cricket, 1900
Croquet, 1900
Golf, 1900, 1904
Real tennis, 1908
Lacrosse, 1904, 1908
Motor boating, 1908
Pelota, 1900
Polo, 1900, 1908, 1920, 1924, 1936
Rackets, 1908
Rugby, 1900, 1908, 1920, 1924
Tug of war, 1900, 1904, 1906, 1908, 1912, 1920

Ever present

Fifteen events have been held in every modern Olympics:

Track and field
100m
400m
800m
1500m
Marathon
110m hurdles
High jump
Long jump
Triple jump
Pole-vault
Shot put
Discus

Fencing
Individual foil
Individual sable

Swimming
1500m freestyle

'Almost events'

The single sculls and coxed eight-oared shell were scheduled in 1896, but cancelled because of bad weather. However, they have been held every time since.

Pole-vaulting

Have you ever wondered about the origins of pole-vaulting? Probably not! There are various theories. It existed as a gymnastic discipline in Germany in the 1790s, and a painting by A. W. Devis, from the same decade, shows an Eton schoolboy pole-vaulting a 6-foot railing. The earliest known competitive pole-vaulting (or 'catgallows with poles' as it was then called) goes back to 1839 when a Mr Alcock cleared 9 feet at Greystoke Races.

An alternative theory is that it was invented in the mid-nineteenth century in Ulverston, North Lancashire, by shepherds who found vaulting the best way to cross streams and ditches. Eventually it became a competitive sport in Cumberland and Westmorland, including the Grasmere sports. Originally, though, the rules allowed a competitor to climb up the pole and jump!

(If pole-vaulting originated in Germany, then the old joke may be very old: 'Are you a Pole, Walter?' 'No, I'm German – but how did you know my name?')

(Sources: Paul Lovesey, *AAA Centenary History*, and Dan Birtwistle, Ulverston Heritage Centre.)

Pole-vault winner

When Wolfgang Nordwig of Germany won the men's pole-vault in 1972, he was the first non-American to win the pole-vault in the modern era. The USA had a 100 per cent record from 1896 to 1968.

Eric the Eel

Eric Moussambani of Equatorial Guinea – Eric the Eel, as he has become known – epitomises what the Olympics are about. He apparently only learned to swim a year before the 2000 Olympics, and had never swum a full 100m race. The other two swimmers in his heat were disqualified for false starts, so Eric swam alone – pretty slowly – but, to the roars of the crowd, he finished! His time was 1:52.72. (The gold medal was won in 48.30.)

Winners and losers

For every medallist there are 17 Olympians who go home empty handed, and behind this bald statistic there are stories of great human tragedy and achievement:

Sad endings
- Andrea Ruaducan, the victorious Romanian gymnast in the 2000 Games, who failed a drugs test and lost her medal – her error was to have taken a cold-cure.
- Vicky Dunn, the British judo player who travelled all the way to Sydney, but failed to make the weight.

Oldest and youngest
- Lorna Johnstone, of the UK, became the oldest ever female Olympian when she completed in the dressage in 1972 at the age of 70.
- Dimitrious Loundrous of Greece was 10 years and 218 days old when he finished third in the parallel bars in 1896.

- Majorie Gestring of the USA won the springboard diving in 1936 at the age of 13 years and 268 days.
- Oscar Swahn was 72 years and 279 days when he took silver in the running deer shooting in 1920. In 1912 he was the oldest-ever gold medallist.

Keeping it in the family
- Russian Irina Nazarova won a relay gold medal in 1980, following in the footsteps of her mother, Elizabeth Bagrinaseva, who took gold in the discus in 1952.
- Willy and Lottie Dod of Great Britain were the first brother and sister to win Olympic medals in 1908.

Team tactics
In the 1908 Olympics in London, the final of the 400m was between three American runners and Wyndham Halswelle of the UK. The Americans used team tactics to block Halswelle and an official broke the tape and declared the race void. The London QOC ordered the race to be re-run, but the American athletes refused to take part. Next day, Wyndham Halswelle ran on his own – to win. Only the gold medal was awarded.

Long careers
- Hurbert Raudaschl of Austria competed nine times in Olympic sailing competitions (1964–96).
- Four Olympians – Magnus Konow of Norway, Ivan Osiier of Denmark, Paul Elvstrom of Denmark and Durwood Knowles of the Bahamas – competed in two (or more) Olympic Games, 40 years apart.

Swimming

The only swimming event in the 1896 Olympics was the 100m freestyle – in the sea off Piraeus. In 1900 at the Paris Olympics, swimming events were held in the Seine – and the competitors' times were fast as the swimmers swam with the current. From

1904, though, the swimming events were held indoors. Women's swimming was introduced in 1912.

Remarkable gymnast

In 1904 American George Eyser won three golds, two silvers and a bronze in gymnastics, all achieved even though he had a wooden leg.

Class issue

J. B. Kelly, Olympic gold medallist rower and father of Princess Grace of Monaco, was banned from competing at Henley in 1920 because he had once been a bricklayer, thus falling foul of the Amateur Rowing Association's rules, which banned manual workers from competing.

Bias

The year 1908 was the last one in which the host country supplied all the officials. This is to avoid accusations of bias by officials – for example, using megaphones to urge on their home team, and allegedly deliberately breaking the tape to force a re-run of the 400m race after a British runner had been beaten.

Marathon!

At the 1912 Olympics in Stockholm, one of the 75-kilogram middleweight Graeco-Roman wrestling semi-finals lasted 11 hours and 40 minutes! The competitors were Martin Klein, an Estonian representing tsarist Russia, and Alfred Asikainen of Finland, who was eventually defeated.

Unfortunately, Klein was too exhausted to wrestle in the final and had to settle for second place.

Talking in class

In 1972, American 400m runners Vince Matthews and Wayne Collett were banned from the Olympics for disrespectful behaviour to the national anthem when receiving their gold and silver medals. The pair chatted on the podium during the anthem.

No medal

In 1900 a local boy was a last-minute replacement as a cox in the coxed pairs rowing team that won gold. He disappeared without trace afterwards and never got his medal.

Shock

Stella Walsh (born Stanislawa Walasiewiczowna in Poland) won the 1932 women's 100m dash. When she was killed in 1980 the post-mortem revealed one big surprise – she was a man!

'Who cares who's third?'

In his excitement about David Hemery's world-record-breaking gold medal in the 1968 400m hurdles, David Coleman shouted out, 'Hemery first, Hennige second, who cares who's third?' Shortly afterwards he had to admit, rather sheepishly, that it was John Sherwood of Great Britain who was third.

Prior to 1904, Coleman would have been right, as only the winner got a medal.

Officially perfect

In 1976 the gymnastics judges awarded Romania's Nadia Comaneci seven perfect 10s.

Killing the competition

When Bob Beamon stepped up to take his fourth jump – following two no-jumps and an average jump – in the 1968 Olympic long jump, the world record stood at 8.35 metres. Beamon jumped 8.90 – this was 55 centimetres further than anyone else had ever jumped. The competition was over, and this world record was to stand for 23 years.

Seven gold medals!

In the 1972 Games Mark Spitz won seven gold medals:

100m butterfly
100m freestyle
200m butterfly
200m freestyle
4×100m freestyle relay
4×100m medley relay
4×200m freestyle relay

Dawn Fraser

The Australian swimmer Dawn Fraser, who won four gold medals in swimming, was banned for 10 years after the 1964 Olympics in Tokyo, when she and some friends celebrated her victory by acquiring the national flag from the Japanese Imperial Palace.

Ancient superstars

Leonidas of Rhodes was the first superstar, winning 12 championships between 164 BC and 152 BC. Milon of Kroton won the boys' wrestling title in 540 BC. He won the senior title in 532 BC and successfully defended it four times before losing in the final in 512 BC to Timasitheos of Kroton.

First woman

The first recorded female Olympic champion was Kyniska of Sparta who won the tethrippon in 396 and 392 BC.

Eight individual gold medals

Ray Ewry of the USA won eight individual gold medals – still a record – including three in the standing long jump and the standing high jump. He won his last medals in 1908.

Ten-goal Sophus

Sophus Nielsen scored 10 goals (football) for Denmark against France in 1908. France had entered two teams and Denmark, who finished second overall, beat their B team 17–1. Amazingly, Gottfried Fuchs equalled the feat for Germany against Russia in 1912.

Longest event

The longest-ever Olympic event was the 320-kilometre cycle race in 1912. The winner, Okey Lewis of South Africa, finished the course in 10 hours 42 minutes 39 seconds.

Avoiding boredom

In 1912 Jim Thorpe won the five-event pentathlon and later the ten-event decathlon. In between, he came fourth in the high jump and seventh in the long jump.

Hero to villain and back

Jim Thorpe, on his return to the USA after winning the pentathlon and decathlon in 1912, was accorded a hero's welcome and a tickertape parade. However, it was then discovered that he had played a few professional baseball games, which disqualified him from amateur status. He was consequently stripped of his Olympic titles. After his death, the IOC reinstated him and presented duplicate medals to his children.

Evelyn Ashford

After coming fifth in the 100m sprint, Evelyn Ashford said, 'Participating in the Olympics seemed bigger than life to me.' She missed the 1980 Games when the USA boycotted the Moscow Games, but in 1984 she won three gold medals.

One way to win

In 1920 Norway won seven yachting events – in five of them there was only one entrant!

Summer and winter

Eddie Eagan is the only Olympian to win gold in Summer and Winter Games – boxing in 1920 and bobsledding in 1932.

That will show them!

The USA did not select Robert Legendre in the long jump in 1924, but only in the pentathlon. However, he broke the world long jump record while competing in the pentathlon.

Author and rower

Ben Spock, of *The Common Sense Book of Baby and Child Care* fame, won a rowing gold in 1924.

Unisex

Men and women compete against one another in shooting, yachting and equestrian events.

First marathon winner

When Spiridon Louis, a Greek postal worker, won the 1896 marathon he was showered with prizes: a lifetime supply of clothes, shaves and haircuts, chocolate, wine, jewellery, sheep and cattle. He was even offered the hand of a wealthy bene-factor's daughter which, however, he refused – being already married!

Ahead of her time

Mildred Didrikson won gold medals in 1932 in the 80m hurdles and javelin. She also broke the world record and finished equal first in the high jump. However, her prototype Fosbury flop – 36 years before Dick Fosbury – was ruled illegal.

The nearly people

Nathaniel Cartmell, Hans Grodotzki, Ivo van Damme and Raelene Boyle each won two silver medals at an Olympics, but never a gold. In 1904 Cartmell lost both sprints to compatriot Archie Hahn, and Grodotzki took silver in the 5000m and 10,000m in 1960. Van Damme came second to Juantorena in the 800m, and John Walker in the 1500m in 1976. Boyle actually got three silvers – 100m and 200m in Munich and 400m in Montreal. Four great athletes, but not an Olympic gold between them.

Greg Louganis

Greg Louganis won the gold medal in the men's springboard diving in 1988 after hitting his head on the board in the preliminary competition so severely that he required stitches.

Sir Steve Redgrave

Everyone knows about Steve Redgrave's five rowing gold medals. However, it is less well known that during the 1989–90 season he was a member of the British bobsleigh team.

'Fosbury flop'

Perhaps the highest accolade for an athlete is to have something in the sport named after you. In 1968 Dick Fosbury won the gold medal in the men's high jump, using a novel technique in which the jumper goes over the bar head first and backwards. The technique so caught on that, by 1980, 13 of the 16 finalists in the Olympic high jump were using the 'Fosbury flop'.

The US coach Payton Jordan's concern expressed at the time – 'Kids imitate champions – if they try to imitate Fosbury, he'll wipe out an entire generation of high jumpers because they all will have broken necks' – proved unfounded.

Over-excited

When Jean Boiteux won the 400m freestyle in 1952, his father was so excited that he jumped into the pool to celebrate!

Worth the wait?

In 1924 Bill Havens was chosen to represent the USA in the rowing but, as his wife was pregnant, he opted to stay with her rather than compete. Some 28 years later that child, Frank Havens, took gold in the 10,000m canoeing!

Close shave

In 1956 the American bantamweight weightlifter, Charles Vinci, found himself 200 grams overweight only 15 minutes before the weigh-in. Savage measures included cutting off all his hair, but he made it and won the gold medal!

Preparation!

Walker Don Thompson was worried about the heat and humidity in Rome for the 1960 Olympics, so he equipped a room in his house with heaters and boiling kettles and trained there! He then won the 50,000m walk.

Amazing finish

In the cycling road race in Rome in 1960, a great pack of riders approached the finish together. After 195 kilometres, Mario Zanin of Italy won the gold medal, while Sture Petterson at the back of the pack took fifty-first place just 0.16 seconds behind the winner.

Bizarre record

Giovanni Pettenella of Italy and Pierre Trentin of France hold one of the most bizarre Olympic records. In their cycling sprint semi-final in 1964 — where the tactics tend to be 'cat and mouse' — the pair stood without moving for 21 minutes 57 seconds!

How long is a marathon?

The answer is 42.195 kilometres (26 miles 385 yards) — the distance from Marathon to Athens. Well, actually it is the distance from Windsor Castle to the Royal Box inside the White City Stadium. This distance was settled at the 1908 London Olympics. The 1908 marathon was 42.2 kilometres and in 1920 the distance was 42.75. Since 1924, the distance has always been 42.195 kilometres.

Appendix 1:
100 Metres Gold Medallists

Men's 100m – Olympic gold medallists

1896 Thomas BURKE (USA) 12.0
1900 Frank JARVIS (USA) 11.0
1904 Archie HAHN (USA) 11.0
1906 Archie HAHN (USA) 11.2
1908 Reginald WALKER (SAF) 10.8
1912 Ralph CRAIG (USA) 10.8
1920 Charles PADDOCK (USA) 10.8
1924 Harold ABRAHAMS (GBR) 10.6
1928 Percy WILLIAMS (CAN) 10.8
1932 Eddie TOLAN (USA) 10.3
1936 Jesse OWENS (USA) 10:3
1948 W. Harrison DILLARD (USA) 10.3
1952 Lindy REMIGINO (USA) 10.4
1956 Bobby Joe MORROW (USA) 10.5
1960 Armin HARY (GER) 10.32
1964 Robert HAYES (USA) 10.05
1968 James HINES (USA) 9.95

1972   Valeriy BORZOV (USSR) 10.14
1976   Haseley CRAWFORD (TRI) 10.06
1980   Allan WELLS (GBR) 10.25
1984   Carl LEWIS (USA) 9.99
1988   Carl LEWIS (USA) 9.92
1992   Linford CHRISTIE (GBR) 9.96
1996   Donovan BAILEY (CAN) 9.84
2000   Maurice GREENE (USA) 9.87

Women's 100m Olympic gold medallists

1928   Elizabeth ROBINSON (USA) 12.2
1932   Stanislawa WALASIEWICZ (POL) 11.9
1936   Helen STEPHENS (USA) 11.5
1948   Fanny BLANKERS-KOEN (HOL) 11.9
1952   Marjorie JACKSON (AUS) 11.5
1956   Elizabeth CUTHBERT (AUS) 11.5
1960   Wilma RUDOLPH (USA) 11.0
1964   Wyomia TYUS (USA) 11.49
1968   Wyomia TYUS (USA) 11.08
1972   Renate STECHER (GDR) 11.07
1976   Annegret RICHTER (GER) 11.08
1980   Lyudmila KONDRATYEVA (SOV) 11.06
1984   Evelyn ASHFORD (USA) 10.97
1988   Florence GRIFFITH-JOYNER (USA) 10.54
1992   Gail DEVERS (USA) 10.82
1996   Gail DEVERS (USA) 10.94
2000   Marion JONES (USA) 10.75

Appendix 2:
A Comparison Between
the Results of 1896 and
Those of 2000

100m

1896   Thomas Burke 12.0
2000   Maurice Greene 9.87

400m

1896   Thomas Burke 54.2
2000   Michael Johnson 43.84

800m

1896   Edwin Flack 2:11.0
2000   Nils Schumann 1:45.08

1500m

1896   Edwin Flack 4:33.2
2000   Noah Kiprono Ngenyi 3:32.07

Marathon

1896   Spiridon Louis 2:58.50 (2 hours, 58 minutes and
       50 seconds)
2000   Gezahgne Abera 2:10.11 (2 hours, 10 minutes and
       11 seconds)

High jump

1896   Ellery Clark 1.81
2000   Sergey Kliugin 2.35

Pole-vault

1896   William Welles Hoyt 3.30
2000   Nick Hysong 5.90

Long jump

1896   Ellery Clark 6.35
2000   Ivan Pedroso 8.55

Triple jump

1896   James Connolly 13.71
2000   Jonathan Edwards 17.71
(In 1896 the event consisted of two hops and a jump.)

Appendix 3: Gold Medallists in Sydney 2000

(Note: Names of team members are listed only when there are four or less.)

Archery

Men's Team 70m: South Korea (Jang Yong-Ho; Oh Kyo-Moon; Kim Chung-Tae)
Men's Individual 70m: Simon Fairweather, Australia
Women's Team 70m: South Korea (Soo-Nyung Kim; Nam-Soon Kim; Mi-Jin Yun)
Women's Individual 70m: Mi-Jin Yun, South Korea

Badminton

Men's Singles: Ji Xinpeng, China
Women's Singles: Gong Zhichao, China
Men's Doubles: Indonesia (Tony Gunawan; Candra Wijaya)
Women's Doubles: China (Ge Fei; Gu Jun)
Mixed Doubles: China (Jun Zhang; Ling Gao)

Baseball

Men: USA

Basketball

Men: USA
Women: USA

Boxing

Light Flyweight: Brahim Asloum, France
Flyweight: Wijan Ponlid, Thailand
Featherweight: Bekzat Sattarkhanov, Kazakstan
Bantamweight: Guillermo Ortiz, Cuba
Lightweight: Mario Kindelan, Cuba
Light Welterweight: Mahamadkadyz Abdullaev, Uzbekistan
Welterweight: Oleg Saitov, Russia
Light Middleweight: Yermakhan Ibraimov, Kazakstan
Middleweight: Jorge Gutierrez, Cuba
Light Heavyweight: Alexander Lebziak, Russia
Heavyweight: Felix Savon, Cuba
Super Heavyweight: Audley Harrison, Britain

Canoe(C)/Kayak(K)

Men's C-1 500m: Gyorgy Kolonics, Hungary
Men's K-1 500m: Knut Holmann, Norway
Men's C-2 500m: Hungary (Ferenc Novak; Imre Pulai)
Men's K-2 500m: Hungary (Zoltan Kammerer; Botond Storcz)
Men's C-1 Slalom: Tony Estanguet, France
Men's C-1 1000m: Andreas Dittmer, Germany
Men's K-1 Slalom: Thomas Schmidt, Germany
Men's K-4 1000m: Hungary (Akos Vereckei; Gabor Horvath; Zoltan Kammerer; Botond Storcz)

Men's K-2 1000m: Italy (Antonio Rossi; Beniamino Bonomi)
Men's K-1 1000m: Knut Holmann, Norway
Men's C-2 1000m: Romania (Mitica Pricop; Florin Popescu)
Men's C-2 Slalom: Slovakia (Pavol Hochschorner; Peter Hochschorner)
Women's K-1 500m: Josefa Idem Guerrini, Italy
Women's K-2 500m: Germany (Birgit Fischer; Katrin Wagner)
Women's K-4 500m: Germany (Birgit Fischer; Katrin Wagner; Manuela Mucke; Anett Schuck)
Women's K-1 Slalom: Stepanka Hilgertova, Czech Republic

Cycling

Men's Madison: Australia (Scott McGrory; Brett Aitken)
Men's One Kilometre Time Trial: Jason Queally, Britain
Men's Keirin: Florian Rousseau, France
Men's Mountain Bike: Miguel Martinez, France
Men's Olympic Sprint: France (Laurent Gane; Florian Rousseau; Arnaud Tournant)
Men's Individual Pursuit: Robert Bartko, Germany
Men's Road Race: Jan Ullrich, Germany
Men's Team Pursuit: Germany (Guido Fulst; Robert Bartko; Daniel Becke; Jens Lehmann)
Men's Individual Road Time Trial: Viacheslav Ekimov, Russia
Men's Points Race: Juan Llaneras, Spain
Men's Sprint: Marty Nothstein, USA
Women's 500m Time Trial: Felicia Ballanger, France
Women's Sprint: Felicia Ballanger, France
Women's Mountain Bike: Paola Pezzo, Italy
Women's Points Race: Antonella Bellutti, Italy
Women's Individual Pursuit: Leontien Zijlaard, Netherlands
Women's Individual Road Time Trial: Leontien Zijlaard, Netherlands
Women's Road Race: Leontien Zijlaard, Netherlands

Diving

Men's Platform: Liang Tian, China
Men's Springboard: Ni Xiong
Men's Synchronised Springboard: China (Xiao Hailiang; Xiong Ni)
Men's Synchronised Platform: Russia (Igor Loukachine; Dmitri Saoutine)
Women's Synchronised Springboard: Russia (Vera Ilina; Ioulia Pakhalina)
Women's Platform: Laura Wilkinson, USA
Women's Springboard: Mingxia Fu, China
Women's Synchronised Platform: China (Li Na; Sang Xue)

Equestrian

Team Three-Day Event: Australia (Phillip Dutton; Andrew Hoy; Stuart Tinney; Matt Ryan)
Team Dressage: Germany (Isabell Werth; Nadine Capellmann; Ulla Salzgeber; Alexandra Simons de Ridder)
Team Jumping: Germany (Ludger Beerbaum; Lars Nieberg; Marcus Ehning; Otto Becker)
Individual Dressage: Anky Van Grunsven, Netherlands
Individual Jumping: Jeroen Dubbeldam, Netherlands
Individual Three-Day Event: David O'Connor, USA

Fencing

Men's Team Foil: France (Jean-Noel Ferrari; Brice Guyart; Lionel Plumenail; Patrice L'hotellier)
Men's Team Epee: Italy (Angelo Mazzoni; Paolo Milanoli; Alfredo Rota; Maurizio Randazzo)
Men's Individual Foil: Young Ho Kim, Korea
Men's Individual Sabre: Mihai Claudiu Covaliu, Romania
Men's Individual Epee: Pavel Kolobkov, Russia

Men's Team Sabre: Russia (Serguei Charikov; Alexei Frossine; Stanislav Pozdniakov)
Women's Team Epee: Russia (Karina Aznavourian; Tatiana Logounova; Maria Mazina; Oxana Ermakova)
Women's Individual Foil: Valentina Vezzali, Italy
Women's Team Foil: Italy (Diana Bianchedi; Giovanna Trillini; Valentina Vezzali)
Women's Individual Epee: Timea Nagy, Hungary

Football

Men: Cameroon
Women: Norway

Gymnastics

Men's Parallel Bars: Xiaopeng Li, China
Men's Team: China
Men's Rings: Szilveszter Csollany, Hungary
Men's Floor Exercise: Igors Vihrovs, Latvia
Men's Pommel Horse: Marius Urzica, Romania
Men's Horizontal Bar: Alexei Nemov, Russia
Men's Individual All-Around: Alexei Nemov, Russia
Men's Trampoline: Alexandre Moskalenko, Russia
Men's Vault: Gervasio Deferr, Spain
Women's Balance Beam: Xuan Liu, China
Women's Individual All-Around: Simona Amanar, Romania
Women's Team: Romania
Women's Rhythmic Individual: Yulia Barsukova, Russia
Women's Rhythmic Team: Russia
Women's Floor Exercise: Elena Zamolodtchikova, Russia
Women's Trampoline: Irina Karavaeva, Russia
Women's Uneven Bars: Svetlana Khorkina, Russia
Women's Vault: Elena Zamolodtchikova, Russia

Handball

Men: Russia
Women: Denmark

Hockey

Men: Netherlands
Women: Australia

Judo

Women's Half Heavyweight: Lin Tang, China
Women's Heavyweight: Hua Yuan, China
Women's Half Lightweight: Legna Verdecia, Cuba
Women's Middleweight: Sibelis Veranes, Cuba
Women's Half Middleweight: Severine Vandenhende, France
Women's Lightweight: Isabel Fernandez, Spain
Women's Extra Lightweight: Ryoko Tamura, Japan
Men's Heavyweight: David Douillet, France
Men's Lightweight: Giuseppe Maddaloni, Italy
Men's Extra Lightweight: Tadahiro Nomura, Japan
Men's Half Heavyweight: Kosei Inoue, Japan
Men's Half Middleweight: Makoto Takimoto, Japan
Men's Middleweight: Mark Huizinga, Netherlands
Men's Half Lightweight: Huseyein Ozkan, Turkey

Modern Pentathlon

Men: Dmitry Svatkovsky, Russia
Women: Stephanie Cook, Britain

Rowing

Men's Eight: Britain
Men's Four Without Coxswain: Britain (James Cracknell; Steven Redgrave; Tim Foster; Matthew Pinsent)
Men's Lightweight Fours: France (Jean-Christophe Bette; Xavier Dorfman; Yves Hocde; Laurent Porchier)
Men's Pairs Without Coxswain: France (Michel Andrieux; Jean-Christophe Rolland)
Men's Quadruple Sculls: Italy (Agostino Abbagnale; Rossano Galtarossa; Simone Raineri; Alessio Sartori)
Men's Single Sculls: Rob Waddell, New Zealand
Men's Lightweight Double Sculls: Poland (Tomasz Kucharski; Robert Sycz)
Men's Double Sculls: Slovenia (Iztok Cop; Luka Spik)
Women's Double Sculls: Germany (Kathrin Boron; Jana Thieme)
Women's Quadruple Sculls: Germany (Meike Evers; Kerstin Kowalski; Manja Kowalski; Manuela Lutze)
Women's Eight: Romania
Women's Single Sculls: Ekaterina Karsten, Belarus
Women's Lightweight Double Sculls: Romania (Constanta Burcica; Angela Alupei)
Women's Pair Without Coxswain: Romania (Georgeta Damian; Doina Ignat)

Sailing

Men 470: Australia (Tom King; Mark Turnbull)
Women 470: Australia (Jenny Armstrong; Belinda Stowell)
Men's Mistral: Christoph Sieber, Austria
Women's Mistral: Alessandra Sensini, Italy
Tornado Class: Austria
Europe Class: Shirley Robertson, Britain
Finn Class: Ian Percy, Britain
Laser Class: Ben Ainslie, Britain

Soling: Denmark
49er: Finland
Star Class: USA

Shooting

Men's Trap: Michael Diamond, Australia
Men's Double Trap: Richard Faulds, Britain
Men's Free Pistol: Tanyu Kiriakov, Bulgaria
Men's Air Rifle: Yalin Cai, China
Men's Running Game Target: Ling Yang, China
Men's Air Pistol: Franck Dumoulin, France
Men's Rapid Fire Pistol: Serguei Alifirenko, Russia
Men's Three-Position Rifle: Rajmond Debevec, Slovenia
Men's Free Rifle Prone: Jonas Edman, Sweden
Men's Skeet: Mykola Milchev, Ukraine
Women's Air Pistol: Luna Tao, China
Women's Sport Pistol: Maria Grozdeva, Bulgaria
Women's Skeet: Zemfira Meftakhetdinova, Azerbaijan
Women's Trap: Daina Gudzineviciùte, Lithuania
Women's Three-Position Rifle: Renata Mauer-Rozanska, Poland
Women's Double Trap: Pia Hansen, Sweden
Women's Air Rifle: Nancy Johnson, USA

Softball

Men: USA

Swimming

Men
50m Freestyle: Anthony Ervin, USA
100m Butterfly: Lars Froelander, Sweden
100m Breaststroke: Doico Fioravanti, Italy
100m Backstroke: Lenny Krayzelburg, USA

100m Freestyle: Pieter Hoogenband, Netherlands
200m Freestyle: Pieter Hoogenband, Netherlands
200m Individual Medley: Massimiliano Rosolino, Italy
200m Backstroke: Lenny Krayzelburg, USA
200m Breaststroke: Doico Fioravanti, Italy
200m Butterfly: Tom Malchow, USA
400m Freestyle: Ian Thorpe, Australia
400m Individual Medley: Tom Dolan, USA
1500m Freestyle: Grant Hackett, Australia
4×100m Medley Relay: USA (Lenny Krayzelburg; Ed Moses; Ian Crocker; Gary Hall Jr)
4×100m Freestyle Relay: Australia (Michael Klim; Chris Fydler; Ashley Callus; Ian Thorpe)
4×200m Freestyle Relay: Australia (Ian Thorpe; Michael Klim; Todd Pearson; William Kirby)

Women
50m Freestyle: Inge De Bruijn, Netherlands
100m Breaststroke: Megan Quann, USA
100m Butterfly: Inge De Bruijn, Netherlands
100m Freestyle: Inge De Bruijn, Netherlands
100m Backstroke: Diana Mocanu, Romania
200m Backstroke: Diana Mocanu, Romania
200m Butterfly: Misty Hyman, USA
200m Individual Medley: Yana Klochkova, Ukraine
200m Freestyle: Susie O'Neill, Australia
200m Breaststroke: Agnes Kovacs, Hungary
400m Individual Medley: Yana Klochkova, Ukraine
400m Freestyle: Brooke Bennett, USA
800m Freestyle: Brooke Bennett, USA
4×100m Medley Relay: USA (B. J. Bedford; Megan Quann; Jenny Thompson; Dara Torres)
4×100m Freestyle Relay: USA (Amy van Dyken; Dara Torres; Courtney Shealy; Jenny Thompson)
4×200m Freestyle Relay: USA (Samantha Arsenault; Diana Munz; Lindsay Benko; Jenny Thompson)

Synchronised Swimming

Women's Team: Russia
Women's Duet: Russia (Olga Brusnikina; Maria Kisseleva)

Table Tennis

Men's Doubles: China (Wang Liqin; Yan Sen)
Men's Singles: Linghui Kong, China
Women's Doubles: China (Li Ju; Wang Nan)
Women's Singles: Wang Nan, China

Taekwondo

Men's Welterweight: Angel Matos Fuentes, Cuba
Men's Flyweight: Michail Mouroutsis, Greece
Men's Featherweight: Steven Lopez, USA
Men's Heavyweight: Kyong-Hun Kim, Korea
Women's Featherweight: Jae-Eun Jung, Korea
Women's Welterweight: Sun-Hee Lee, Korea
Women's Flyweight: Lauren Burns, Australia
Women's Heavyweight: Zhong Chen, China

Tennis

Men's Doubles: Canada (Sebastien Lareau; Daniel Nestor)
Men's Singles: Yevgeny Kafelnikov, Russia
Women's Doubles: USA (Serena Williams; Venus Williams)
Women's Singles: Venus Williams, USA

Track and Field

Men
100m: Maurice Greene, USA
110m Hurdles: Anier Garcia, Cuba
200m: Konstantinos Kenteris, Greece

400m: Michael Johnson, USA
400m Hurdles: Angelo Taylor, USA
800m: Nils Schumann, Germany
1500m: Noah Kiprono Ngenyi, Kenya
3000m Steeplechase: Reuben Kosgei, Kenya
5000m: Millon Wolde, Ethiopia
10,000m: Haile Gebreselassie, Ethiopia
4×100m Relay: USA (Jonathan Drummond; Bernard Williams; Brian Lewis; Maurice Greene)
4×400m Relay: USA (Alvin Harrison; Antonio Pettigrew; Calvin Harrison; Michael Johnson)
Marathon: Gezahgne Abera, Ethiopia
20km Road Walk: Robert Korzeniowski, Poland
50km Road Walk: Robert Korzeniowski, Poland
Decathlon: Erki Nool, Estonia
Discus Throw: Virgilijus Alekna, Lithuania
Hammer Throw: Szymon Ziolkowski, Poland
High Jump: Sergey Kliugin, Russia
Javelin Throw: Jan Zelezny, Czech Republic
Long Jump: Ivan Pedroso, Cuba
Pole-vault: Nick Hysong, USA
Shot-put: Arsi Harju, Finland
Triple Jump: Jonathan Edwards, Britain

Women
100m Hurdles: Olga Shishigina, Kazakstan
100m: Marion Jones, USA
200m: Marion Jones, USA
400m Hurdles: Irina Privalova, Russia
400m: Cathy Freeman, Australia
800m: Lurdes Mutola, Mozambique
1500m: Nouria Benida Merah, Algeria
5000m: Gabriela Szabo, Romania
10,000m: Derartu Tulu, Ethiopia
Marathon: Naoko Takahashi, Japan

4×100m Relay: Bahamas (Sevatheda Fynes; Chandra Sturrup; Pauline Davis-Thompson; Debbie Ferguson)
4×400m Relay: USA (Jearl Miles-Clark; Monique Hennagan; Marion Jones; La Tasha Colander-Richardson)
20km Road Walk: Wang Liping, China
Discus Throw: Ellina Zvereva, Belarus
Hammer Throw: Kamila Skolimowska, Poland
Heptathlon: Denise Lewis, Britain
High Jump: Yelena Yelesina, Russia
Javelin Throw: Trine Hattestad, Norway
Long Jump: Heike Drechsler, Germany
Pole-vault: Stacy Dragila, USA
Shot put: Yanina Karolchik, Belarus
Triple Jump: Tereza Marinova, Bulgaria

Triathlon

Men's Triathlon: Simon Whitfield, Canada
Women's Triathlon: Brigitte McMahon, Switzerland

Volleyball

Men's Beach: USA
Men's Indoor: Yugoslavia
Women's Beach: Australia
Women's Indoor: Cuba

Water Polo

Men: Hungary
Women: Australia

Weightlifting

Men's Lightweight: Galabin Boevski, Bulgaria
Men's Middleweight: Xugang Zhan, China

Men's Featherweight: Nikolay Pechaliv, Croatia
Men's Light Heavyweight: Pyrros Dimas, Greece
Men's Middle Heavyweight: Akakios Kakiasvilis, Greece
Men's Heavyweight: Hossein Tavakoli, Iran
Men's Super Heavyweight: Hossein Rezazadeh, Greece
Men's Bantamweight: Halil Mutlu, Turkey
Women's Flyweight: Tara Nott, USA
Women's Featherweight: Xia Yang, China
Women's Lightweight: Soraya Mendivil, Mexico
Women's Middleweight: Xiaomin Chen, China
Women's Light Heavyweight: Weining Lin, China
Women's Heavyweight: Maria Isabel Urrutia, Colombia
Women's Super Heavyweight: Meiyuan Ding, China

Wrestling

Freestyle Flyweight: Namig Abdullayev, Azerbaijan
Freestyle Bantamweight: Alireza Dabir, Iran
Freestyle Featherweight: Mourad Oumakhanov, Russia
Freestyle Lightweight: Daniel Igali, Canada
Freestyle Welterweight: Alexander Leipold, Germany
Freestyle Middleweight: Adam Saitiev, Russia
Freestyle Light Heavyweight: Saghid Mourtasaliyev, Russia
Freestyle Super Heavyweight: David Moussoulbes, Russia
Greco-Roman Bantamweight: Armen Nazarian, Bulgaria
Greco-Roman Flyweight: Kwon Ho Sim, Korea
Greco-Roman Lightweight: Filiberto Azcuy, Cuba
Greco-Roman Featherweight: Varteres Samourgachev, Russia
Greco-Roman Welterweight: Mourat Kardanov, Russia
Greco-Roman Middleweight: Hamza Yerlikaya, Turkey
Greco-Roman Light Heavyweight: Mikael Ljungberg, Sweden
Greco-Roman Super Heavyweight: Rulon Gardner, USA

Further Reading

Eric Liddell

Eric Liddell, Ellen W. Caughey, Paperback Barbour Publishing, Inc., 2000.

God's Joyful Runner, Russell Wilcox Ramsey, Bridge-Logos, 1998.

Complete Surrender, Julian Wilson, Monarch, 1996.

Eric Liddell: The Making of an Athlete and the Training of a Missionary, D. P. Thompson, The Eric Liddell Memorial Committee, Glasgow, 1945.

Scotland's Greatest Athlete: The Eric Liddell Story, The Research Unit, Crieff, 1970.

Eric H. Liddell: Athlete and Missionary, D. P. Thompson, The Research Unit, Crieff, 1971 (same book as *Scotland's Greatest Athlete*).

Eric Liddell: Running for God, Sue Shaw, Openbook, Adelaide, 1993.

Eric Liddell, Catherine Swift, Bethany House, 1990.

Eric Liddell, David McCasland, Pure Gold, 2001.

The Flying Scotsman, Sally Magnusson, Quartet Books, 1981.

Eric Liddell: Something Greater Than Gold, Janet and Geoff Benge, YWAM, Seattle, 1998.

Chariots of Fire and a Christian Message for Today, W.J. Weatherby, Jim Ryun and Anne Ryun, Harper & Row, San Francisco, 1983.

Story of Eric Liddell (video), RBC Ministries, Grand Rapids (90 minutes).

Michelle Akers

Michelle Akers, with Judith A. Nelson, Success Factors, 1996.

The Game and the Glory: An Autobiography, Michelle Akers with Gregg Lewis, Zondervan, 2000.

Michelle Akers: The Game of Her Life (video), RBC Ministries, Grand Rapids (18 minutes).

Jonathan Edwards

A Time to Jump (The authorised biography of Jonathan Edwards), Malcolm Folley, HarperCollins, 2000.

More Than Champions (video), CTA, 1996 (40 minutes).

Kriss Akabusi

Kriss Akabusi on Track, Ted Harrison, Lion, 1991.

Kriss, Stuart Weir, HarperCollins, 1996.

Amanda Borden

Magnificent Seven: The Authorized Story of American Gold, Amanda Borden, etc., Delacorte Press, 1996.